SHINE ON YOU CRAZY DAISY
- VOLUME 4

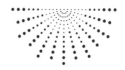

COMPILED BY TRUDY SIMMONS

CONTENTS

Printed in the United Kingdom First Printing, February 2022

ISBN: 9781739914868 (paperback)
ISBN: 9781739914875 (eBook)

The Daisy Chain Group International Ltd
Hampshire, UK
connect@thedaisychaingroup.com

Book Cover Design: Gemma Storey from Infinity Creative
Photo Credit of Trudy Simmons: Nisha Haq Photography

This book is dedicated to....

....All the businesswomen that are showing up and putting themselves out there to be seen and heard. We are all in this together... this is for you to take inspiration, that we are all on a similar journey, but taking different paths, with varying bumps along the way to here.

You can do it! Keep going!

Shine Bright and Shine On.

ACKNOWLEDGMENTS

This is to acknowledge and appreciate all of those that have contributed and shared a piece of their journey with us all in this book. Thank you for your courage and tenacity. You are all inspirational.

As you will read in this book, success is different for everyone. The way that we decide what success means to us, and how we get there, is a culmination of 1000s of choices and decisions that we make in our businesses.

Each of these brilliant businesswomen have shared a part of their journey and each of us knows, that we can't do it alone, we aren't meant to do it alone. Surround yourself with the people that "get it".

To the Facebook communities that I run – Hampshire Women's Business Group and International Women's Business Group for showing me each and every day that whatever we are going through, we are all there for each other. For being the communities that we all call "our lounge-room" where we come to share, ask for help, support, advice and give from our expertise without expectations. I am grateful for the "tribe" that we have and that like attracts like. Community is everything on this lonely road. Come and join ours, it is the best – tee hee!

I stand for inclusion on all aspects. The baseline of everything that we build, is on kindness and being available with open arms to all businesswomen that wish to be a part of something and want to be seen and heard. We are here for all of that.

Welcome.

INTRODUCTION

This book is about creating a platform for businesswomen to have an inspirational voice and to share their stories with others, to show that this entrepreneurial rollercoaster is the highs AND the lows and that we navigate them all differently, but hopefully with a tribe/team of people that support our vision to our success – whatever that looks like, and it is different for everyone.

Each story is unique, each story is REAL, each story offers a piece of insight, motivation and encouragement when we need it the most. You are not alone.

These are un-edited chapters of real stories from women that have been where you are and have stories to share about how to find your way, not feel isolated, find out what you CAN do, rather than feeling stuck in what you think you can't do.

Here…. Are their stories!! Bong bong…

Charity donation

As we gain, so can we give – that is my philosophy of running my own business. 10% of the profits from this book will be donated to the bereaved families of the NHS who have died while looking after us and our families during the Corona-Virus pandemic.

To find out more, or to donate, please visit this website –

www.healthcareworkersfoundation.org

THE CHOICE... IS YOURS!

Trudy Simmons

L et's start this book with a statement: I was miserable. Miserable because I had been working so hard, doing the things, speaking to people, thinking about the people I hadn't spoken to, thinking about the things I hadn't done.

I was miserable.

I had a business coach who I reached out to in (what felt like at the time) desperation. I NEEDED something. But I didn't know what that was, or how to feel better or how to DO better.

I did the usual (I'm sure you understand) whinging about "why wasn't this working?", "what did I need to do next?", "who did I need to speak to?". And then she asked me (I'm sure you are on the edge of your seat by now!): "What do you want the business to be? What are you aiming for? What direction do you want to go in?".

I stopped. I thought. I started to speak, and like all of us at some point, I said, "I don't know".

Now, I am not the kind of person who stays with "I don't know". I need to know, I need to find out, I WANT to do better.

But what actually happened is I tried to fill the space/moment with babble – have you done that? I started to speak nineteen-to-the-dozen, filling the space with words that were literally just jibber-jabber of why I didn't know and what I didn't know and why this was all too hard for me to work out – pfft – what a crock!

That day, 10 years ago, I made choices and decisions that have set my path for continually growing, changing and adapting my business to always be what I WANT it to be. And I was able to do this because I created the clarity, direction and ultimately, the focus to always aim for what I wanted to build.

How did I do this?

Clarity is a hum-dinger of a start! Without the clarity of what you're building, you can't create the direction you're going in, and without the direction you're aiming for, you don't know WHAT to focus on – is this making sense??

Let's start at the very beginning; it's a very good place to start!

Clarity

What do you want your business to be? What do you want it to give you? What do you want it to offer? What makes you HAPPY? What makes you SHINE? Why do you want it to grow? Why do you want to work so danged hard for yourself and your potential clients?

Give yourself the opportunity to answer these questions and find out the basis for what your business really is.

For me, I was born to entertain... in case we haven't met, I am hilarious (winky face emoji!). I want people to feel happy. Happiness breeds motivation, and we all need to be and feel motivated to move towards accomplishment.

My brain is also very practical and productive. My past careers were in Operational Management – I used to run teams of brilliant, motivated people who could fix the wheel on an office chair or build specifications to write computer programmes. I can see the big picture and the very next step to take – and then help with the steps in the middle to make sure you achieve your clarity and direction. This is how I help and work with my clients.

Once I realised these things, I became clearer on what I wanted to do and who I was IN that. I started to make decisions about what I wanted the business to look like and what success looked like for me. And for me, it was (and has always been) seeing people's faces spring to life when their businesses are aligned with their happy (quick... trademark that!!).

I love to listen to people, take everything out of their head, give it a little shake and make sure there is nothing left to say, and then put the pieces back together in a way that makes sense, in a way that we can all say, "I get it now, I see what I want". THAT feeling is priceless and essential to creating a solid foundation to build a future on.

And once I did this for myself, I found my happy, I found my clarity, I found my purpose. Eek.. I just wrote "purpose" and felt icky – the word can be so overused these days in a business sense, but honestly, it is what happens. Whether you're creating a painting and watching the recipient appreciate the art, or giving people the space and time to be seen and heard – your feeling of "this is what I am meant to do" is in there; it is just a question of finding it.

Once you know what that feeling is, and that it makes you happy and it's a product or service you can offer – find your direction!

Direction

Crikey. You now have the clarity and motivation of what you want to build and why you want to build it. READY?

Picture the scene. Shut your eyes and see the path ahead of you, with the end result/goal at the end of the path. Can you see it? What does the path look like? Is it cluttered with the debris of your past? Does it have lots of other commitments, distractions, potential procrastinations in your way?

I know when you're reading this, there are things popping into your head that are in your way – write those critters down. These are the things that are helping you to play small and stay stuck – BE GONE – we have got things to do!

On the side of our path (which hopefully is becoming less cluttered!) are our competitors, our "they have copied me" people, the "why aren't I as successful as them" colleagues – but make sure that they are on the side of your path – WHY?

STAY IN YOUR LANE! When we allow our direction to become intertwined with what other people are doing, other people are saying, other people are achieving, we lose sight of OUR clear path. Kick 'em off your path, they don't need to be there getting in the way of your Clarity!

And now… (drum roll please) we have the clarity and direction of what we're working towards. We have cleared the distractions. We need… wait for it …. FOCUS!

Focus

OMG… I see you procrastinating, fiddling, flaffing and falarfering. We've all been there. "I'll just go and watch this episode on Netflix, THEN I will be ready and able to get back to it" – and then the inevitable "where did that 4 hours go??" RIGHT??!!

Here's the thing (and this is the tough love, hard-arsery that I am known for) and I hope you're sitting down. You either want this, or you don't. You either work towards it, or away from it. You either take the ACTION or you wonder why it isn't happening. You either let all the gumpf get in your way, or you kick it to the kerb and clear your path.

What do you CHOOSE? And it is a choice.

I know you want this; I know you see what you can do – GO DO IT!

Creating focus and accountability is essential to the continual and consistent growth of your business.

Working ON your business, rather than in your business is how businesses grow. I was asked recently what the difference was, and this was my response: "working IN is the 'job' part of what you deliver. Working ON is being the CEO, looking at the big picture, making sure you are growing, learning and planning".

Not giving yourself the scheduled time to focus on the bird's-eye view leaves you paddling like a little duck – serene-social-media like on the top and your feet paddling so fast under the water that you feel like you can't breathe.

Schedule in the committed time for yourself to look at your business, get focused back on the clarity and direction and get accountable to creating and doing what you need to move towards your future.

Remember at the beginning of the chapter when I said that I was miserable? Well guess what – I TOOK ACTION. I looked at all the parts of my business. I made decisions and choices – because it is my business and I can do that! I let go of a few things that weren't working for me. I cancelled services that were not making me happy; I changed my approach to my working week. I took action on being focused and kept the picture in my mind (and actually on a cork board in front of me!) of a clear path, and to the best of my ability, even now, I kick the distractions, energy-vampire-people and extraneous I-must-get-this-done-but-I-don't-want-to things OFF MY PATH. I keep my path clear (or at least clearer... or at least some days... or at least 1 day a week – ya know… we are all human!) so I feel like I can achieve what I WANT to achieve, grow what I CHOOSE to grow, do what I WANT to do. And if (and when!) things get in the way, I can make conscious decisions to either sit, wallow and throw a tantrum (and I'm pretty sure you know that this happens!) OR, I can decide to take action, hold myself accountable and FOCUS.

As Cilla Black used to say, "The choice… is yours".

BIO:

Trudy Simmons is a Clarity and Productivity Business Coach for women entrepreneurs, with a truckload of empathy and a little bit of hard-arse! She helps you find out WHAT you want to do, WHY you want to do it, and HOW to get it DONE! She loves to show her audience how to become more successful by getting clarity, taking action and following through. Trudy has 20 years' experience in helping people move from being stuck and not knowing the next step, to getting their shizzle DONE by finding and harnessing their strengths and removing their weaknesses! She knows what keeps you up at night – the thousand ideas that are germinating in your brain – and she knows how to sort them into "no go", "maybe later", and "hells yes", and get done what is really important to your success. She is the creator and founder of the Shine On You Crazy Daisy membership – the opportunity to grow your tribe, expand your audience, take in monthly knowledge, work ON your business in online co-working and focus and accountability fortnightly group coaching.

www.thedaisychaingroup.com

2

THE LIE ABOUT 'SUCCESS'

Dominique Mullally

I, like everyone, thought that 'happiness' was a destination and 'success' was a measure!

It's an outcome.

A house.

A car.

A relationship.

A high powered job.

A high income.

You know… something you aspire to 'have'!

Surely that makes you happy!

But it took me 31 years to realise, we've all been sold a lie!

I've been a high achiever since as far back as I can remember.

I was driven to be the best that I could be.

I was competitive not against others, but against myself and I constantly raised the bar as to what I could achieve. My earliest memory of this stems from when I was about 6. It started with laps in the swimming pool. See I grew up in Australia. Think long summers, hot days and salty sea air. Every school holiday my friends and I would spend our time in the pool. We invented this game where we would pretend we were mermaids, and we would have to hold our breath and swim underwater from one end of the pool to the next for as long as we could. Whoever did the most laps, won! I wasn't really 'successful' at first but as time went on, I became unbeatable! I would push myself each time and refused to surface for breath until I knew I had pushed myself to my limit. Going beyond my comfort zone and stretching myself. Pushing myself each and every time proving to myself and everybody else that I was the best. To achieve that title of winner, at being successful!

Even if it was just swimming laps in a pool.

But that's where it started, that need to challenge myself continuously and to push myself and it is still a trait I possess today.

I think it's an amazing characteristic to have, however it can also be detrimental when you allow it to unconsciously rule your life, seeking the next thing and the next thing to prove your 'worth' or seeking validation.

My love of money and 'success' led me into financial services.

I remember as a kid seeing people drive big fancy cars or have big fancy homes and my inner thought was always, how did they get that? What was it that made them so 'successful' and I, along with many others, made the association that success came from things.

Things are what you should aspire to obtain and money is the way in which you get it! And all of that makes you happy, right?

And so I remember receiving money for the 1st time and 'feeling' like money made me happy. Like it was something I wanted to strive for.

And strive for it I did, over the next 25 years!

I have always been ambitious. Always driven and as I've

already shared, someone who likes a challenge! So if someone told me I couldn't have something, or something couldn't be done, or that reality was impossible, you bet I'd find a way to prove you wrong!

And I did, many times over.

I accomplished more at 31 than most people have in a lifetime.

I had the 'he's not real' fiancé because he was just 'too' perfect.

I had the 'oh my god' ring which was valued at more than most would spend on a home deposit.

I had a beautiful home 10 mins from the most beautiful beach you've ever seen!

I had the 'high powered' role as an Independent Financial Adviser.

I had my own business.

I had a 6 figure income.

I had a portfolio of assets that secured my future.

I had 'it all' right?

I was now officially 'successful' and therefore, happy right?

Wrong!

I hated my life. I was fucking miserable!

From the outside looking in, I had all the materials anyone would want, I was 'successful' by society measurements but what I didn't have was peace. Peace in my mind or in my heart, to know that I was truly happy. I certainly didn't 'feel' successful!

I used to look around at others and feel envious when I saw them light up with their partners. I mean what was wrong with me?

I had a man who had the biggest heart and would do ANYTHING for me. He'd given me the ring I'd dreamed of and he constantly went out of his way to surprise me and to do things to make me happy and yet here I was, miserable as sin!

I had a job and a business that paid extremely well, but being quite often the only woman in a room full of men, I felt the need to continuously prove my worth. I had to be 'better' than the male advisers because I had more to prove. I was extremely masculine in my energy and it led me to feel continually stressed and eventually burnt out.

My weekends were spent wining and dining at some new restaurant, and for anyone who knows me, they know food is one of my biggest pleasures and yet that only filled a temporary void.

I would be at the beach, in the water, any spare second I had. Even that wasn't enough to wash away the guilt and shame I felt for being so bloody ungrateful for my 'amazing' life.

But by who's definition was it 'amazing'?

I started to see myself beyond my current reality and ask, is this it? Is this what life is supposed to be about?

I've achieved the 'stuff' so why aren't I happy?

And then, my life imploded! My relationship with the 'perfect man' broke down and I had to start to reassess my life beyond the plan.

You know the 'plan' we all have for how our lives' 'should' be! I'd already begun to question it but now I had the opportunity to really reassess it because now it was all about me! However, I felt like an absolute failure!

But a failure by whose standards?

The truth is... we've been sold a lie about happiness, success and failure that keeps most subscribed and indoctrinated to a system that is not fit for human purpose nor spirit!

We're conditioned from an early age to believe that 'success' is measured by things and stuff, you know, all the 'tangible' things you can see and/or touch.

It's in the money you make, the title you have, the car you drive, the house you live in, the holidays you take, the dreamboat partner that everyone loves – all of that right there tells society how 'successful' you really are!

So people spend their whole lives chasing the 'stuff'.

Failure and success are infact byproducts of social expectations.

We're taught what 'should' bring us happiness and what you 'should' go after to be successful and if you don't achieve those 'you're a failure' a 'loser' in life.

What a load of bullshit!

As a result of these narratives and expectations, I had subscribed and conformed to a life that wasn't my own. I mean yes of course it was 'my own' but I had created a reality and a construct of a world that was built upon the ideals of others. I created metrics for my 'successful' life without truly understanding what brought me true happiness and peace.

I was suddenly in a position where I had to face a reality that I couldn't escape. My perfect, successful life had imploded before my eyes and now I was faced with a choice. Was I going to continue to walk this path of where I thought I was going, or use it as an opportunity to redefine my notion of success?

I had become so far out of alignment with who I truly was and what fed my soul, I no longer recognised who I was. So I closed down my book of business, sold all my possessions and said goodbye to my life in Australia.

For the first time in a long time, I had no plan for the future. I felt liberated and free. Not having a plan can be terrifying or it can be this enormous opportunity to redefine your life and success based on who you REALLY are once you've stripped away the material aspects of what defines success.

I chose the latter.

I then spent the next 7 months travelling the world and pushed myself out of my comfort zone in more ways than you can ever imagine and it was the best form of self development I could have ever done. With no home or job to go to, no partner to rely on, no day to day distractions to take me away from my thoughts, I spent hours, days in fact, in silence with nothing but my thoughts and stripped down bare to truly understand the core essence of who I was and what I wanted for my life?

I had to really define what made me truly happy and what was 'Dominique's' definition of success going to be? What was that construct and reality I wanted to create and the word that came up over and over again was Freedom.

Freedom to choose.

Freedom to be.

Freedom to express.

Freedom to explore.

Freedom to authentically live my life based on my terms and definitions of what success looked like.

Freedom to be truly happy!

I had it all and I gave it up for the freedom to be happy and successful on my terms. Life is not a dress rehearsal, we only get one shot so live your life and construct a reality based on your definition and expectations for the life you want to create.

Don't allow your life or your business to be defined by the expectations of others.

Create your own definitions of success, happiness and failure.

Take risks, be bold, be true but most importantly be authentically you and build your business and your life in alignment with your highest values!

BIO:

Dominique Mullally is a Business Growth Strategist & Consultant and founder of Financially Fierce Females. Dominique helps women in business build, grow and scale their business using her proven Wealth Accelerator Framework to maximise sales, increase cashflow, grow profits and build real wealth. Dominique uses her expertise in Financial Advising, NLP, EFT and Hypnotherapy combined with her own experience of creating Financial Independence for herself, to empower women with the mindset and strategies of how to use business and other income producing assets as wealth creation vehicles to multiply income and profits to create time, emotional and financial freedom. Dominique is a published author and on a personal mission to inspire as many women as she can to become Financially Empowered, Unapologetically Successful.

www.instagram.com/dominiquemullally

3
JOY IN THE JOURNEY

Joanne Bonnett

J ust curious: how many times in your life can you pinpoint a moment of impact, knowing exactly how you felt, where you were and what happened next? This is the story of a moment which dramatically changed the direction of my life's journey ... and it started, somewhat appropriately, on a train.

I found a seat. Flipping miracle! I was still out of breath. I'd left my office on Baker Street "early", ran to the station in knee-high black patent stiletto boots carrying my laptop & over-stuffed handbag, tripped on the escalator and almost broke my neck but *actually* snapped the heel off my boot. Always running somewhere. Trying to catch up with myself before I arrived wherever I was meant to be next. If I didn't make THIS train I'd be late to pick up my boys from after school club. Again. I'd pushed through my first ever panic attack on the platform (that's a whole other story!) and somehow willed my out-of-body self onto the Tube.

Hallelujah, I'd made it. The 5:24 from Waterloo. Breathe.

Then... (assume sneery, nasal tone of voice)

"We are sorry to announce the late departure of this train due to a points failure at Wimbledon."

Stay calm. Keep breathing. Tim's away on business. Call a friend, you've got a network for this. The other working mums get it. Call another friend. And another. No can do. So sorry Jo...

I dialled Mum by reflex. But she wasn't there anymore and I remember being grateful I was sitting down when the world dissolved around me and I disappeared into a pool of grief. There's nowhere lonelier than a crowded place when your heart's breaking and everyone around you avoids eye contact. Where were all the humans??

Something. Has. To. CHANGE. I can't keep doing this. WHY am I doing this?

Don't get me wrong, I was grateful for my lucrative corporate career in IT. I'd worked hard but there came a point where travel was just tiring, the pace became pressure, success turned to stress and I couldn't shake the feeling there was more to life. I wanted to put my family before my boss but how on earth could I get off this train to start a new journey and travel in a completely different direction? I'd followed the right map, hadn't I? Do well at school, Uni, career, house, married, kids, doing it all, having it all, juggling it all but terrified something was going to drop and smash ... I knew it was time for a detour.

So I jumped off the train. Not literally and not immediately but in a moment of clarity (the exact number of days between my notice period and the start of the school summer holidays!) I resigned with no plan B other than trusting my instincts. It was so easy in the end. It FELT right. Have you ever noticed that once you make a decision and act on it, everything starts to make sense? It's the overthinking that eats us up!

Well, that was 14 years ago. And oh my goodness my train has been on a different track since then and I've been driving!!

It's a good thing I didn't have a plan because if I had, it definitely wouldn't have included the Global Financial Crisis and going from two good corporate incomes to ZERO. I have faith and a strong belief that there is always a silver lining ... and that became clear one bleak winter lunchtime when Tim and I were at the kitchen table realising what a JOY it was to see more of each other, to be there for the boys & all their activities (they were 8 and 11), to see daylight every day, to NOT be commuting, to choose our holiday dates without asking permission, to laugh more. Presence really was the gift that kept on giving. There's always a catch though. We couldn't keep doing this without earning an income. And SOON.

In any situation there are only two things we can control: our attitude and our activity. The quick and easy answer was to go back to freelance marketing consultancy, so I did. And instantly felt the soul-sucking pull of the black hole I'd so happily spun away from.

I was organising a charity ball, publishing the church newsletter, freelance work, supporting Tim with his new business (we both knew it was time to ditch having a boss!), helping a friend launch her new business ... I was BUSY but serendipity surprised me with a whole new journey.

No such thing as a free lunch? Well I had a very rewarding 'free' lunch at a business event called 'What's Stopping You?' where I'd hoped to find some freelance opportunities but instead something completely different popped into my path.

"Would you like to try this vegan skincare?"

errr... "No, not really, I've got sensitive skin ... and is it one of those 'things'??"

"Well, what if these products could be the route to a sustainable, ethical way to grow a flexible business from home? Are you even curious? Open minded enough to have a chat?"

Well the rest, as they say, is history. I got over myself, my preconceived ideas about an industry I actually knew nothing about, asked myself "What if it works?" ... and then I got to WORK!

One thing I know for sure is when you combine a strong work ethic with a dash of inspiration and a desire to create the change you want to see, magic happens. Spoiler alert: it's not actually magic. I've lost track of how many times people have told me I'm 'lucky' but isn't it interesting how lucky we can be when we work with passion and purpose?

Fast forward a year from making the jump and I was redefining what success looked and felt like in my life.

I was reading more, listening more, learning more, laughing more, connecting more, creating community and before long I was even earning more. Who knew? What if the rest of your life could be the best of your life?

Software to skincare? That wasn't the big leap. The big leap was trusting that nudge inside, the deep knowing there could be more to life if I dared to dream … and then working to make it happen.

So if you're reading this, I don't know where you are in your journey, which train you're riding and whether you've even got a clue where you're going. I do know that if you feel like you aren't in control of the speed, the direction or you aren't enjoying being around your fellow passengers then maybe it's time to get off at the next stop, take a look around and decide where to go next.

I still love this definition of 3-Dimensional success that anyone can fit to their own dreams and desires and check in with it regularly:

- TIME: freedom to spend it with whom you want, doing what you want, when you want
- MONEY: a sense of peace that there is enough, you've got it covered
- SERVICE: making a difference and a positive impact

Let's fast forward again to today. There have been many miles travelled, a couple of dark tunnels, plenty of maintenance, regular refuelling, lots of incredible views, some stop signs but we've kept looking for the green lights. Our boys are now both in their 20s and loving life. We were present as a family during those school years and they saw first-hand the results of hard work. Tim and I now run several businesses from our home. There's always something to be grateful for and new adventures on the horizon. My hair may be silver now – but that too, like so many changes, has been a positive and empowering choice.

I realised along the way that what really lights me up is connecting people with their passion and purpose and helping them discover their unique gifts and talents.

I started learning about The Enneagram and trusted that familiar nudge inside to pursue this new adventure and bring it along for the ride! What even is that? The Enneagram is an ancient system of personality that helps us to connect our mind (how we think), our body (what we do) and our heart/spirit (how we feel) – taking a holistic approach to understanding who we are, what motivates us and how to respond to ourselves and others. Mentoring people to find their own lightbulb moments is quite the buzz! Isn't it wonderful to be open to whatever surprises may be waiting for us around the next bend?

One of the biggest wins has been my mindset shift. When I jumped off the old train I was bruised, broken and drowning in self doubt. I'm humbled when friends who know me today comment on my positivity, bounce-back-ability, attitude of gratitude and focus on finding the silver lining. Even when we think we're failing we are growing and learning.

Have there been ups and downs? Of course – at times it's felt like a rollercoaster and life keeps happening no matter what. I often had to remind myself that other people's opinions were not going to pay our bills. Digging deep became familiar territory and I realised that sometimes to have what you want in the longer term there have to be sacrifices in the short term.

If I was to start this journey again, knowing what I know now and the lessons learned along the way, what would my advice be?

It's not all about the destination – find your joy in the journey because when you develop an explorer's heart you will want to keep discovering what's next.

- Make time to pause, enjoy the view and celebrate the wins along the way
- Reset your course if you need to – success is rarely a straight line
- Pick up new travel companions, value them - and let some leave!
- It's ok to change pace ... just keep moving forward
- You can't pour from an empty cup – refuel yourself regularly

You're stronger than you think – it's amazing how a tiny seed of an idea, watered with a sprinkling of belief can grow into something beautiful. If you're doubting yourself, overthinking, feeling unsupported, not sure what to do next then truly, I've been there. You can always get in touch, I'd love to cheer you on YOUR journey and I'm pretty sure that someone, somewhere is already watching you, willing you to succeed and being inspired by you.

Go on, it's time to buy your ticket. Step on board and let's do this!

. . .

BIO:

'Be who you were created to be and you'll set the world on fire' - by St Catherine of Siena. For years I focused on the 'fire' part but that just led to burnout (!) in my corporate marketing career. Realising that being truly YOU is the best place to be was when everything made more sense. Now my passion lies in working with wholehearted women who dare to dream the best is yet to come... and together we make midlife and beyond the best time of our lives ...

Here are a few ways I could help you:

- Guiding you towards healthier habits for Mind Body Skin and Life
- Mentoring you in a global online business to create sustainable lifestyle change
- Helping you discover who YOU were created to be with The Enneagram
- Encouraging you to find your Silver Linings

www.joannebonnett.com

4
I'M NOT OUT TO CHANGE THE WORLD

Sam Winch

For a long time I harboured a feeling of guilt around my business success.

My newsfeed is flooded with links to articles like "7 Reasons why the "why" is so important" from Forbes, or "Why we need a why: the importance of purpose" by Eurni.

I often hear the discussion around the importance of knowing your WHY, the driving force behind why you started your business. How it's vital to have a purpose, something bigger than yourself, or more than just the money. Something to keep you going when times get tough.

But discussions like this used to make me feel guilty and ashamed.

I didn't know my why. I didn't have a grand vision of helping people or changing the world. I didn't start my business to cure world hunger or bring around world peace.

In fact, I started a business, and have been completely self-supported by it for 9 years now, almost by accident. I didn't have a grand plan, I didn't wake up one morning with a vision, or a driving purpose. Instead, when something wasn't working for me and my family, I took the next step in front of me to make a change. Sometimes it worked, sometimes it didn't.

Step by step, it's led me to the business success I have today. But I felt like I couldn't call myself a success without a motivating mission. I left school with no idea what I wanted to do in the world. I signed up for a dual degree at a local university, but I quickly worked out university isn't a great place to be if you have no idea what you want to do, and don't love the courses you are doing. I dropped out after just 3 months and picked up a casual job in a large retailer. By the time I was 24 I'd made my way up to General Merchandising Manager and was responsible for millions of dollars of turnover. But (there's always a but) I also had 2 young children. Working late nights, overnight shifts, weekends and public holidays is hard work, especially with a young family. When my first born was just one, I found myself working so late on Christmas eve that I had to send his grandma to collect him from day care. The mum-guilt was strong, and I knew something had to change. Being back at work again by 6am on Boxing Day really cemented those feelings. My next step came seemingly accidentally. I was offered a role as a face to face trainer that I never would have thought to apply for (and that I wasn't qualified for) which ended up being the perfect fit for my skills. But (see, there's always a but) I had a 2 hour commute into the city each day, and as I worked my way up the team, the hours were long. So I started doing some of my own consulting on the side of my training role, meeting with business owners to talk about my background in sales, business management and face to face facilitation and gradually my consulting work replaced my training work. Using these skills I created a company that developed and delivered face to face training, and all was going well. Then I got divorced, remarried, and had 2 more babies. I still vividly remember trying to rock a 5-day old baby in one hand, and finish a company compliance report with the other, because the audit had a tight deadline and as the CEO I was the one who had to sign off on the report. Again, I realised that something had to change.

I closed the company within the following month and opened a consulting practice that built online courses for other training companies and businesses. This gave me the opportunity to use my learning and development skills, without having to deal with the delivery, facilitation, and day to day compliance of courses. It gave me the freedom to work in the hours that suited me, around the kids, and everything else that came with my life at that point. That freedom and flexibility has served me successfully to this day. I make a great income, spend my days building amazing courses for some awesome business owners, and couldn't imagine ever going back to working for someone else. At each decision point along the way, I felt like I just took the next step in front of me.

I didn't have a huge driving WHY.

I didn't jump off the deep end. I didn't "go all in". I don't have motivating stories of the day I realised I was going to change the world. I simply made the decision that felt best for me and my family at each step of the journey.

I love the flexibility of doing my own thing and spending more time with the kids (and to be honest, I think I would make a terrible employee now), but I've often felt huge guilt around not having some motivating mission.

I felt like I "should" have one, like everyone else had one, and that I didn't.

It wasn't until a discussion with a business friend several years later, that I began to realise what I was all about.

I mentioned to them that I was attracting some awesome clients. Clients who really get me, clients who are open and honest, clients who are practical and realistic, clients who tell me things they would normally be embarrassed to tell other people. Clients who don't care if I rock up in flip flops (because I will) or if I swear (because I will).

He asked me what allowed me to attract these clients…

And I responded: Me

I really embraced just being me.

I let go of the feeling that I had to be "professional". That I needed to wear certain things or look a certain way. I let go of the feeling that I had to build my business a certain way, I didn't fit the "funnel" model, I didn't do sales calls, and I didn't hard sell.

I leaned into the things that I felt good about doing and serving my clients the way I wanted to be served.

I started just being me, really me. The nerdy, inappropriate, casually dressed me.

I started sharing more about me. I started being more honest about life, about the ups and the downs of business, and about how I get things done.

And suddenly I realised… this is part of my why.

My why is because I don't want to have to fit into someone else's box anymore. Turning up at their defined hours, sitting in an office all day, doing things their way, just doesn't work for me. My why is because as a mum of 4 kids, with a husband in the Defence Force, and still closely co-parenting with my ex-husband, flexibility is the key to making my life work.

My why was me, but that felt like a selfish answer.

For so long I'd been told that I had to have an external driving force, an intrinsic want to help others, that admitting to myself that I'm in it for me felt selfish.

But really, it's my ultimate form of self-care.

It allows me to earn a great income and still be there for my family. It gives me the flexibility to work around everything and everyone. I simply don't see how any job with fixed hours, or long commutes could work for me.

And as an extension of that, I want others to realise that it's possible for them to.

I want you to realise that you can just be yourself, that you can live your life in your own way and that you can build the business that suits you. Not the business you think you should build, not the one everyone on the internet tells you that you have to build, not the funnel that everyone else is using. Just the bits you want, the way you want.

I want people to feel free to show their true self, not hide behind a mask, or a "professional" exterior.

I want them to know that it is all ok. That none of us really have our shit together (it just looks like that from the outside) and that we are all making up this thing called "adulthood" as we go along.

I want them to know that their social media doesn't have to be perfect I want them to know that everyone fights I want them to know that everyone feels down sometimes I want them to know that there is no "normal"

And that we are all just human.

My WHY isn't about building online courses as such, that is just a vehicle I use to help people get to where they want to be.

Don't get me wrong, my team and I build great courses and help others do the same.

But I truly believe that there isn't only one way to build a successful business, and while courses suit some business models, they won't suit others.

At the end of the day, I want you to be you. I want you to be proud of who you are.

To feel confident to build your business your way. Doing the things you love, and using the strategies that you feel good about, not the ones that someone else tells you that you should be using.

I want you to feel that it's ok to build your life your way.

It is ok not to have a world changing WHY.

You don't have to stand for something huge.

You don't have to want to build a huge brand, or influence millions (although if that's what you want to do, that's awesome too).

But the truth is, your version of success is all about you. Success to you might be paying all your bills. Success to you might be going on holiday. Success to you might be supporting a small team (all of my team are mums working in regional Queensland, and I love that I can give them the opportunity to earn money on their terms, in an area where finding other work might be difficult).

You don't need to have a world changing vision or message.

I didn't start my business with a big why.

But now, I get to do things my way.

And I wouldn't change my version of success for anything.

BIO:

Sam helps busy service providers take all of that knowledge out of their head and turn it into an online course, so they can stop working so many face to face hours.

With over 10 years' experience in face to face and online courses she's worked with a range of industries, including training members of the Australian Defence force, Emergency Services, and Surf Lifesaving Foundation.

With a variety of qualifications in Training Design and Development up her sleeve, she knows how to make the process quick and easy, so you can leverage the time you work and have a bigger reach.

If she's not busy creating courses or pulling all of that wisdom out of your head, then you'll find her kid wrangling and making terrible sandwich related puns about her name.

www.contentintocourses.com.au

5

KNOW WHICH WAY THE WIND BLOWS

Olivia Marocco

I've often been told I'm a 'free spirit' but to be honest, I've never been sure what that meant as it seems such a trivial way to categorise a complex being.

As I prepared to write this story and after googling and some introspecting, I got the gist and could identify with a lot of the signs and character traits that mean I most probably am one – and that may provide some answers as to why I've made certain choices along the way.

I'm an artist at heart with a creative mind and love expressing my personal style in the things I do.

I have a wanderlust and am innately curious about the world, people and cultures. If I could, I'd drop everything to live on a beach in Bali!

I tend to challenge convention and am not particularly interested in being the 'good girl' and maintaining the status quo (sorry Mother).

I don't seek routine and function better when left to my own devices, working on my timeline and playing by my own rules (being my own boss was almost an inevitability).

But when I'm asked to deliver, I do so 110% percent. I'm hard-working, fiercely loyal and do everything with determination, heart and endless passion.

Perhaps therein lay some of the reasons why my personal and entrepreneurial paths have criss-crossed and taken me on some interesting journeys, often in unexpected directions.

Let's rewind to where it all began

I was born in France to an English mother moulded by an affluent, middle-class and traditional British upbringing. She was also a teenager of the sixties, had character and defied convention at that time by falling in love with a Frenchman at the age of eighteen, marrying him and moving to France. My father was young too and studying to be an architect. He came from a huge, Catholic, close-knit working-class family.

My brother and I arrived in rapid succession, spending an idyllic childhood in the countryside near Paris, surrounded by vast numbers of family members, friends and much-loved canine companions. I've been told that I was an exhausting child as I didn't sit still and was always up to mischief.

My genetic mix came from two completely opposed worlds, which inevitably pulled away from each other. My future took on a whole new direction.

My parents divorced in my early teens and I moved to the UK with my mother and brother. I did well at school, despite my poor English and the disruption in my education, then studied in London for a degree in interior architecture; the nearest I could get to my childhood dream of becoming an architect like my father.

. . .

Enter my free-spirited nature

Whilst at uni, I was heavily into the London music and party scene when the French Minister of Culture invited different countries to participate in the Techno Parade, a new initiative to celebrate the electronic music culture. I'd always been good at managing creative projects and contacted the biggest techno club in London inviting them to take part. A year later, I was on my float in the streets of Paris dancing in front of half a million people and dressed like a cyber Statue of Liberty!

It got me thinking. Did I want to spend my life working behind a drawing board? Absolutely not. I wanted something different but didn't know what - yet. Nevertheless, I earned my bachelor's degree in 2000 and set off to discover the world with my then boyfriend, backpacking around Southeast Asia, Australia and New Zealand. I had the most incredible, life-changing experiences.

My mother bought me a second-hand Olympus camera to take on the trip. I'd done a bit of photography as part of my degree and really enjoyed it. Now I could test out those skills in real situations. My love of photography was born and I discovered I actually had quite a talent for it. But I put that thought on hold for a while.

It was time to grow-up

Back to London and real life. I got a job as a marketing executive working for a start-up in the gaming industry. It was a good place to begin a successful corporate career and I was earning decent money. But something kept bugging me. My 30th birthday was approaching, my ten-year relationship was going nowhere and I wanted to spark change in my life. I needed to find my purpose and had to make some tough decisions. Even for a free spirit, reinvention is no easy feat.

I reconnected with my French roots. Farewell London.

Bonjour la Côte d'Azur. I based myself in Nice and created 'Olivia Marocco Photography' as my first business venture. I had a small portfolio of work to showcase, no real business model, some basic branding and a very rudimentary website which I designed myself (in the days before the rise of social media). I started knocking on doors.

Lady Luck was with me!

A chance encounter with a renowned event photographer based in Marseille resulted in a fully booked diary of incentive and corporate events and exciting trips around the world, camera in hand and a healthy bank balance to boot!

International agencies and blue-chip companies hired me to do all manner of gigs. I photographed famous celebrities, royalty, politicians and business leaders. I even hosted events on stage and TV. It was a good life and it continued happily like that for a number of years - but it wasn't all plain sailing.

Discrimination in the workplace, sexism and industry stereotypes have contributed to a general lack of opportunities for women in photography and the profession remains stubbornly male-dominated. As the only female corporate photographer in the region, I had to build my reputation and stand my ground, especially when dealing with macho, local technical and production teams. Event photography is very physically demanding. I toughened up and proved myself to be one of 'lads.'

I thought my future was all mapped out

Then a series of events happened which set me off course. I fell head over heels in love - he was perfect, on paper (you know what's coming!). Dreams of settling down, creating a home in the sun, starting a family were not meant to be. I eventually reached the conclusion that we didn't share the same future vision.

Next, the world was hit by the disastrous 2008 financial crisis and I saw all my event bookings cancelled in a matter of weeks, with little or no compensation. To top it all, I had rekindled the relationship with my father while back in France and we were getting close again, but he fell seriously ill and passed away a few weeks before his 60th birthday. I mourned my father, my shattered love life and the wonderful career I had worked so hard to build. But I've never been one to give up.

Financial survival came with the creation of a new business targeting a flourishing wedding industry. I developed a signature, fine art style and sold my services to local wedding planners whose wealthy, high-end, international clients were coming to the French Riviera to get married. In just a few years, I built my business back up.

But the winds were a-blowin' again

My 40th birthday was casting shadows. A few romantic flutters hadn't resulted in anything serious and my biological clock was ticking. I had never intended to miss out on motherhood, so after a lot of soul searching, I decided to embark alone on the journey of artificial insemination at a reputable Harley Street clinic and to move back to the UK, where my support structure was centred so I could give myself the very best chance of success.

I was fit, lean and healthy and had a good supply of eggs just waiting to meet a soulmate. Sadly, it didn't happen and after a few years of trying, I decided to stop. I'll pass over that period, but it's important to include it in my story as it was the deciding factor in my return to the UK.

I was introduced to the concept of personal branding photography, which didn't exist in France, but made absolute sense. 'Shoot & Share Personal Branding Photography' was launched in 2019 (an awful name really, but I liked it at the time!).

The new business was going well and I was building a strong brand and identity when the pandemic hit. Once again, all my corporate events, weddings and personal brand photography came to a standstill. I joined local online networking groups and was introduced to many wonderful business owners in similar circumstances. It was a truly eye-opening experience to listen to their struggles or learn from those further ahead in their entrepreneurial journeys.

Among them was Tam Goldsmith, a talented brand designer. We connected and an idea grew to combine our unique set of skills, experience and personalities as brand specialists in our own fields to help others - while keeping ourselves visible. We created #BrandYou2020, a private Facebook group. We found brand experts, influencers and thought leaders who were willing to give free insights, advice, support and content to help take the stress and struggle out of creating something new, pivoting an existing business or taking it online. We held weekly interviews, ran peer-powered brand education sessions, shared ideas between fellow business owners and heard about members' brand stories and journeys.

I'm so proud of what Tam and I achieved in just a few short months. Personally, it got me 'out there,' I met dozens of women from all walks of life and every kind of business and learnt so much from them too.

I rebranded and renamed my photography business 'Brand You Photography' and took the legacy of #BrandYou2020 one step further by exploring an idea that had been in my mind for a while; bringing together creative individuals and contributors to produce a publication that shared knowledge, showcased innovation and was modern, real life and fun.

. . .

Where there's a will, there's a way

'Brand You Magazine' was launched online in October 2020 and became a subscription-based print and digital publication in May 2021. It's beautifully designed (all my own work) – in fact, it has even been likened to "Vogue for brands" and is the ultimate monthly gorgeous guide to female entrepreneur success as a boutique brand or small business. There's nothing else like it and it's been creating quite a buzz since the outset. I've got a small team of wonderful helpers and plenty of exciting plans in store for Brand You in 2022. Watch this space!

As I reflect on my path to success so far, one thing I've learnt is that you need to let some things go before they hold you back and hinder you achieving your dreams. I know that outside forces can bear down and disrupt things but I've always stood tall and kept moving forward. I recognise that I tend to walk to the beat of my own drum, but if I can live a happy and productive life with intention and aligned to my values - and make some decent money along the way to reach that beach in Bali - that's just fine by me.

BIO :

Olivia Marocco is the founder and editor-in-chief of 'Brand You Magazine' and the face behind 'Brand You Photography'. She has over 18 years' experience working with innovative business owners, event agencies, large multi-national corporations and small boutique brands. She has created a publication specialising in the very best of must-have branding essentials. Olivia is based in Hampshire and divides her time between the UK and France.

www.brandyoumagazine.co.uk

6

FROM KNOCKED-UP AND
JOBLESS TO MAKING MILLIONS

Gemma Went

S o, there I was, seven months pregnant, a planned first-time
single mum at the ripe old age of 42, and all of a sudden I
was jobless.

F***************ck.

Prior to this defining moment I was doing well, thank you
very much. I'd been a director at a couple of London agencies.
I'd run my own marketing agency for a couple of years in
deepest darkest Soho. Things were rosy. But life has a habit of
throwing curve balls, and I felt like I'd had a whole box of them
thrown at me at once.

After the initial 'why me' moments, I realised that nobody
was going to come to save me from this dire situation, and I had
to crack on and sort it out myself. I decided I wasn't going to let
a little blip like this get in my way, so after hours (and hours) of
emotional crying (well I was seven months pregnant), I hatched
a plan.

A great friend offered to put me up in her guestroom while
my flat was rented out, as I had no other financial support at

that time. I quickly created a new business using all the knowledge I already had, doing what I found easy at that time — which was digital marketing and social media consulting. I set-up a website and optimised it for search so people could actually find me, reached out to everyone I knew to tell them I would be offering my services in a few months' time. Then popped off to pop out a gorgeous baby boy.

Feast and famine to recurring income

I managed to take a few months off to learn how to be a mother and loved every minute. But as single mum who wanted to create enough of a salary to rent our first home, soon I was sat on that bed in the sunny guestroom, baby on the boob, laptop on the bed. I was literally single-handedly creating what would later become a successful business that made millions helping other women to set up their own online businesses, just like I was doing.

I took my first client when my son was 3 months old, by the time he was 9 months old I had secured enough recurring revenue in the business to pay me enough to rent a lovely two up two down. Recurring revenue was something that I prioritised and still today, many years later, is the centre of what I teach my clients. Why? Because when you lock in recurring revenue for at least six months, well those anxieties around where the revenue is coming from disappears and you're no longer a slave to the feast and famine ferris wheel.

Managing a new business and a new baby alone wasn't easy. I worked when he slept. I felt guilty most of the time that I wasn't doing either of them very well. My mind was on overdrive, but as I look back I can see that I did a great job. So many of us are too hard on ourselves, berating our efforts, self-flagellating when actually we should be self-congratulating. I was no different.

After a couple of years, the business was already creating annual multi-six figures and the journey I'd been on to get to this point created a deep desire to help other women create their own independence with an online business. My business had turned my life around and opened up so many new possibilities. It allowed me to work when I wanted to. It allowed me to be around for my kid. It created the flexibility to be able to work as little or as much as I liked. It created a salary that meant I could easily support us both, and later help support my family after I met my, now, husband.

Happily knee deep in tech

Moving from working as a consultant in a one to one capacity with clients, to an online business mentor working at scale was exciting. It felt like a whole new world opened up to me. I've always been a bit of a nerd about and fascinated by technology, so getting knee deep in new tech that you could use to automate an online experience was right up my alley. I dived in.

I created my first online program, an academy with loads of trainings on how to create an online business. I created my first mastermind where I brought a group of women together to grow their businesses with my guidance. I created my first course and sold it again and again passively.

I spent a lot of time researching and learning new methods. Yes I had a lot of experience before I entered the online world, but I truly believe that you never stop learning, and being humble enough to know you don't know everything is a trait I admire. I connected with people in global communities I would never have had access to before. It was exciting.

I created my podcast, *The Simply Smart Business Show*. I won the Entrepreneurs Champion award at the NatWest Great British Entrepreneur Awards. I was being asked to speak on stages, be a podcast guest, and write articles. My personal brand was growing, and things felt easy.

Until they didn't.

Running a race I didn't want to enter

The thing is, with all the excitement and opportunities that come with the booming online business world, came a few downsides. Within this online world is what I call 'The Online Race'. The race to be more, to achieve more, to make more money. When success like this is opened up to us, it can trigger old wounds that make it never enough. So the race continues, as each runner in the online race eyes up the others, sees what they've achieved and wants the same, because they think that they don't have enough yet. They don't feel enough yet, and when your race is based on feeling enough, you'll never get to the finish line.

It's a race nobody can win, because in the end it leads to burnout as our bodies, minds, and souls struggle to keep up with the endless attacks on our nervous systems and mental health from comparisonitis, imposter syndrome and online trolling that are part of this crazy world.

This is what happened to me, and things started to feel less rosy. Sure I'd created millions in my company, I'd created millions for my clients, I had the dream home and a new husband, life was amazing. But my poor body was broken and burnt out. I'd pushed and pushed so hard; I just couldn't keep up. I was constantly fatigued and exhausted yet struggled to sleep as my adrenaline was spiked. I was barely spending enough time with my family as I was always working and struggled to stop as it felt like an obsession. I constantly got ill as my immune system was shot. All in all, I wasn't great to be around.

I'd seen this happen in the corporate world; I'd seen it within the agencies I'd worked at. I never thought it would happen in this space where we run our own business because, well, nobody else is pushing us to do more, there is no boss to answer to. But what inevitably happens is that you become your own boss from hell. Pushing for more, wanting more, making you work long hours.

Perspective and focus

I took a step back and saw it all for what it was. The Online Race, the need for more, the triggered wounds from childhood that were laid bare and open, needing to heal. So I spent the next two years re-evaluating, replenishing, and renewing. I worked with therapists to heal deep trauma being in the online world had brought to the surface, I went on a journey to heal my body from the various issues caused by pushing for six years. I looked at how I wanted to show up and lead in a space full of such opportunity and wonder but that could so easily damage people.

I went on a journey of researching, of learning new skills to understand how I could be part of the solution in this online world I loved so much. I became a certified mindset coach and energy practitioner, giving me the skills to be able to help my clients heal those things that could lead to burnout or mental health issues themselves. I stopped many of my services and doubled down on a few that would teach how to build an online business, while prioritising body, mind, and soul. I looked at what was being taught and how it could be improved to be more inclusive and sustainable, which led me to creating my own Online Business Consultant Certification, where I teach others how to do what I do with my frameworks and processes.

It was a two year journey of ripping everything apart, and then putting it back together again to support people who enter the bright lights of this online world and help them to avoid what I'd been through.

Through all of this, my love for this online business industry never faded. Yes there's a darker side to it, but the opportunities far outweigh that. There has never been a time when it's so easy for women to create financial independence, wealth and legacy for themselves and their families. There has never been a time when it's so easy to set up a business and start making money within months. There has never been a time when the costs of setting up a business is so low that there's no barrier to entry.

This still excites me and being in a position to mentor, coach, teach and guide women through this process in a supportive, sustainable way is my focus. I believe this online business world will open the door to so many more women who want to make big changes in their lives, who want to make a difference. We've barely scratched the surface of what's possible, and I'm excited about what women will achieve in this online space and the knock-on effect that will have on their daughters and their granddaughters as old societal paradigms are broken down and new ways of creating financial independence become the norm.

Now my focus is building my company, The Lighthouse Business Academy, as we shine the light on simple, sustainable ways to create profitable businesses online without burning out or selling out. My legacy is in showing women what's possible, helping them to turn their lives around with a successful business and certifying a new wave of Online Business Consultants.

Not bad for someone who started this thing in a guestroom with a baby and a laptop.

BIO:

Gemma Went is a multi-award winning Online Business Mentor, Certified Mindset Coach, Energy Practitioner and Founder of The Lighthouse Business Academy®. With over two decades of experience across brands, corporates, agencies and small business, Gemma now focuses on helping online business owners create sustainable, profitable businesses. At the core of her work is her Soul Led Success Framework® where she merges online business strategy, mindset modalities and energetics to help online entrepreneurs take their business to six, multi-six and seven figures with a range of courses, programs, and an accredited certification that trains others to become an Online Business Consultant.

www.gemmawent.co.uk

7

FROM HIGH HEELS TO HIGH VIS

Cat Ardi Brennan

Come on in! I've just made a pot of tea to share. Actually on second thoughts, I have a bottle of shiraz so let's crack that instead. Get comfy – use one of the pillows or rugs I have scattered around on my couch while we sip wine and have a good ole' fashioned chinwag about all the things that motivate, scare and inspire us.

There has been one recurrent theme throughout my life, especially in my younger years. This emotion can masquerade as anger, sadness, feeling blue or complete rage. That emotion is fear. Yes, that terrible F-word which is the worst F-word of all.

Early in my career I was a business banker at one of Australia's largest financial institutions. I couldn't believe my luck! I was only 21 years old and working with a large team of experienced bankers, some of whom had been in banking longer than I had been alive. With my laptop suitcase and my sky-high heels, I felt like I was 10-feet tall and bulletproof. Being in the bank was such an exciting time as I was learning so much, meeting new people and really helping people's dreams come true by helping them either buy a new business or expand existing ones.

The lessons I learned just by listening to people's stories and the sheer passion they had for their chosen field was inspiring. I also had some extremely talented managers around me, and today I still reflect back on lessons they taught me. I was able to take away great leadership skills in snippets from each of them so when the time came, I would implement them with my staff. It isn't so much the course of action I took away, but how they made me feel. And that is a huge take away – **we won't always remember the fine details of situations but we will always remember how people made us feel.**

Need for change

With this great role within the bank came great responsibility and cue to stress! After being in the bank for 6 years, I started to burn out. As much as I loved my job, I could sense something inside me, that gut feeling, that I needed a change. Not only that, I felt like all of my clients had inspired me so much by fulfilling their dreams that I was ignoring the signs literally right in front of me. I wanted to create something great, but I just didn't know what at the time.

Working for myself and creating a team excited me, but it also filled me with fear. I had a great job with a great salary, company car and all the works, but it just didn't feel right after a while. The burnout intensified. It was as if my body was physically resisting going about my routine; it was failing me. I began to get severe migraines and sudden onset heart arrhythmia episodes that were unexplainable. My body was stopping and I either had to take notice or continue to punish myself. Fear was keeping me in the bank even though every part of my body, mind and soul needed a change.

When we can't take the wheel for ourselves, this is where

our friends and family can give us clues and possibly a lifeline. During this time, my close friends would come over unannounced to pry me out of the house to get sunshine when I couldn't do it for myself. Accepting help and being vulnerable at this time was one of the hardest things I've ever had to endure, but I see now how letting people care for me when I simply couldn't was necessary. They did the work of guardian angels.

One particular Friday evening while I was out for dinner with my boyfriend, Matt, and friends, I had an urgent client call and stepped outside. Well, 45 minutes later everyone was finished with their meals and getting ready to leave, while my meal remained on the table. I was defeated in this moment. I wasn't present in any capacity and enough was enough. It was time to make a change.

Matt said that no job is worth this much stress and that he agreed it was time to make that change. We'd only been seeing each other for the best part of 6 months, but for him to care for my welfare so much already, it meant a lot.

I jumped into the unknown

So I parked my fear in the pit of my throat as I emailed my manager to tell him of my intention to resign, which was one of the hardest moments of my life. But I knew it had to be done. I jumped out into the unknown with no job to go to, but a knowing that it would all be ok. No matter how low I was, I always knew that I would figure something out to pay the bills.

Matt had been in Australia about 6 months before I met him in 2012. He's from Galway in Ireland, and was hiring earthmoving equipment here and there through his newly created company, Excavation Equipment. Once my last day at the Bank was done, I sat with Matt and looked over his invoicing to try to learn his trade.

Matt has a real knack for sourcing equipment and finding

work for them, but his invoicing was all done by hand. Gradually I moved all of the business invoicing and systems onto the computer and into the Cloud, began to help write tender submissions for contract work. I even built the first website we ever had. This freed Matt up to do what he did best, while I took stock of the operations.

It was just us two in the business to begin with, then we hired a diesel mechanic so we were a party of three. While I didn't know the difference between a tilt tray and a side tipper, my experience from the bank helped me understand the business's finance and the importance of having systems in place. While Matt worked in the business, I worked on it. I swapped my high heels for high visibility shirts and got to work!

Mel Robbin's, American lawyer and author, speaks about acting on inspiration in her book, *The 5 Second Rule*: 'If you have an instinct to act on a goal, you must physically move within 5 seconds or your brain will kill it. .... hesitation is the kiss of death.' Elizabeth Gilbert also talks about a similar theory in *Big Magic* where she says "an idea will come to you and if you don't take action to start to bring it to fruition, the idea 'jumps' and will find someone else to bring it to life. Ideas are easy to miss, often because we aren't paying attention".

While I didn't create the idea for Excavation Equipment, I really wanted to succeed and create something amazing with Matt. So for one of the first times in my life, I took action and I never looked back.

The first two years of business were by far the hardest but we continued as we created a dream together to build a sustainable business for the future. Sustainability and excavation equipment hire and sales may sound like they don't go hand in hand; however, we ensured that our machines were low in emissions and that a portion of profits went into Australian wildlife charities and nature conservation initiatives.

Somewhere amidst all the chaos, Matt and I found a tiny bit

of time to become husband and wife. It isn't always easy working and living together, and the notion of work/life balance is a fallacy. However, we stop talking about work at 7pm, and we always try to work in separate places in our yards. I am mainly in the office, while Matt is mainly in the yard. We're quite fond of one another, but we don't need to be looking at each other all day every day!

We made sure our growing staff members were paid before we were, and sometimes we were late on our rent or wouldn't replace a tyre on our vehicles to save money. It's quite a funny joke still to this day how I drove around on a space saver tyre for months and had to pump it up every second time I drove anywhere. These were the sacrifices we just had to make, and I wouldn't change it for anything as I believe it builds character and also shows that your priority is the business and the people who work for you.

Challenging archaic thinking

While we were busy building our business, I came up against a lot of archaic ways of thinking from other people, mainly older men who would flat out refuse to speak to me because I was 'just the wife,' which is a term I still despise to this day. Rather than simply letting acts of the tongue go, I would pull people up and explain that I can assist with the issue right now, or you can call Matt and he will tell you to speak to me.

The lesson here is – **demand respect.** We all deserve respect – it's a basic human right and no one should tell you otherwise. So while I understand there are generations of people who subscribed to a certain way of thinking, it's our job to continue to correct them when they are wrong and bring them up to speed. Confrontation is healthy and we should all be more honest in the workplace and in general. I'm not talking about a guns-blazing row, but just challenging with respect and healthy dialogue.

Growth

As time went on, we employed more staff and grew from that team of 3 to 20. Matt became the Key Accounts Manager and I became the General Manager. As I worked on the business and looked after our people, Matt worked in the business over-seeing sales, freight and auctions. We're lucky to have amazing people in our business who treat their roles with the utmost integrity and treat Excavation Equipment as if it were their own. It's been a great privilege to lead a team, and I take great responsibility for their professional and personal growth.

I am also proud to say that from that very small beginning around our kitchen table in 2012 to 2022, we have created a $50m business that has multiple yards around Australia. Excavation Equipment has been listed on the Fast 100's Fastest Growing Businesses in Australia since 2015, we've ranked 50/1000 of the fastest growing businesses in Asia Pacific in 2018 and won numerous national and state awards.

And me? Well I won Business Woman of the Year in 2017 and Toowoomba Chamber's Future Leader of the Year in 2019. Not too bad for a girl who was bound by fear just a few years before, eh?

I went from being immobilised by fear to embracing it with gusto because I was done with waiting for the right time. I also decided to embrace the notion of just really not giving a f*ck about what people thought of me – whether I was competent, or had 'earned the right' to speak or have a seat at the table. Making progress in life is far better than being stagnant and I was truly ready to embrace whatever came at me and whatever I chose to chase.

Whilst I say this, of course manners have a place. I wasn't

out there without a filter and raising anarchy. I just chose to step outside of the constant self-reflection and concern about what people thought of me, which is just so exhausting on its own. What people think of me is really none of my business, so I chose to focus on how I felt about myself. From intrinsic actions such as supporting our local charities and being available to speak at events in aid of raising funds for those less fortunate, to just being present for my family and friends as best I can.

My takeaways from my little yarn to you

Remember that you have an impact on the people you meet. Emotional intelligence and making people feel good, inspired, appreciated, etc. is the most important intelligence of all.

Women need to sing their praises more. Don't downplay your achievements. If you don't sing your praises, no one else will.

Don't be afraid of confrontation– mindful honesty is constructive. No more suppressed emotions.

Demand Respect – you deserve it. It is your birthright.

Take action. What's the worst that can happen? You fail and try again, or you succeed the first time round. Back yourself.

.   .   .

Thanks for stopping by for a wine and a chat! I hope I inspired you in some way to follow your gut and live without fear. Remember, everyone deserves a seat at the table and there is plenty for all to eat and eat well.

BIO:

Cat Ardi Brennan is the General Manager of Excavation Equipment, a Sales & Logistics Business based in Australia. When she isn't trying to steal the last piece of Brie on a sharing platter whilst you're not looking, Cat treads the boards at Toowoomba Repertory Theatre and also has a keen interest in all things skincare, travel and her local community. Oh, and Brie and Shiraz.

Cat lives in Toowoomba with her husband Matt and Ziggy Stardust, the Ruby Cavalier.

www.exeq.com.au

8

UNLEASH YOUR INNER ADVENTURESS

Josie Truelove

Have you thought there must be more to life?
Are your circumstances holding you back from something you'd love to do, but can't see how it's possible?

I'd love to share my story with you about how I realised my dreams and achieved things I never thought possible.

Moving from being employed to self-employed was a big step, as I gave up a good salary, but I would never have had the amazing times that I did if I hadn't taken this step in starting my own business.

My intention was to help people achieve their greatest hearts' desires and through my complementary therapy business, I have been able to help people with their mental, emotional and physical issues which were holding them back from living their best life.

Complementary therapies with mindset and meditation is a huge passion of mine, as well as horses and traveling. I never realised how my three passions would come together and offer such wonderful life experiences.

There are times where I thought I'd taken a wrong direction but these have become my greatest learnings. Throughout my journey I have always continued helping people to gain new perceptions in life, grow in confidence and achieve their hearts' desires.

Three years ago my life changed, dealing with bereavements, family health issues and then came the pandemic. Everything changed, but change allows new ideas to blossom and this enabled me to expand my therapy business to a wider audience globally online, offering meditation and mindset coaching. It's exciting to take these opportunities, to grow and move forward.

The Unknown

From school I never really knew 'what' I wanted to do. When I was eighteen, I saw an advert for an au pair in France at an equestrian centre. This saw my inner desires spark. I love horses! I spent the next seven years in France, buying my dream horse and teaching people how to ride.

Back in the UK, aged 25, I again had no idea what to do. What well paid job could I do with no specific qualifications? Then I saw an advert promoting cabin crew jobs on the airline. A few months later, I was flying around the world, helping holiday makers relax, feel safe and enjoy their flight. It really was a fantastic job.

One day, another advert led me down my next path to join the police force, which would offer me more security and better pay. If I could go back in time, this is one decision that I do question, but it gave me everything I asked for, with a secure salary, good benefits, and I was helping people. I received great training and valuable experiences from working on inner city streets to investigating serious crime as a detective. I also got married, bought a house and travelled the world. Now, I could afford to pay towards my next dream and I qualified as a complementary therapist, in Reiki, Reflexology, Massage, Meditation and Mind Detox.

The police force was not for me as I was an innocent country girl having to work in a very intense inner city world, seeing the worst of life on a daily basis. I was dealing with people

who hated and judged you, I had to face my fears and also, I was caught up in the money trap. Where else could I earn this money and have job security with benefits of sick pay, holiday pay and double time.

Life's Lessons

I believe you can never take a wrong path, just a different one. The police force took away my innocence in life where I became less spontaneous and looked at life through a different lens. More fearful, judgemental, lacking confidence, and afraid of getting it wrong, which can have serious consequences as a police officer! My desire was still to help people experience happiness, peace and enjoy life. Luckily, training in complementary therapies and meditation helped me to be aware of and resolve this fearful way of thinking. When you can see your fears and your limiting beliefs you can choose to change them. I learnt to keep moving through the good and bad parts of life to become a better and more compassionate person in helping others.Life is happening and I discovered that it's how you choose to think about what's happening that determines your experience. Not the actual experience.

Moving Forward

"Remember that sometimes not getting what you want is a wonderful stroke of luck"
Dalai Lama.

I love this saying, to trust and know that there's always something else.

I decided to follow my heart and set up my therapy business, leaving the security of full time employment in the police. Life is too short to be unhappy.

Wanting to travel, my husband and I bought a camper van, known as the fluffy bus, and off we went to France, turning left at Calais with no other plans. What a brilliant adventure we had. Selling the fluffy bus twelve months later, a friend offered us a beautiful farm cottage to stay in. Again, this was perfect timing and I started up my new business as a therapist. But how could I have a business as a therapist and still travel? Then, as before, I saw an advert aligned with my wishes, asking for mobile massage therapists. Perfect timing, so working with a fantastic team of therapists I traveled nationwide to all types of events, festivals and also abroad.

Now having my own business as a therapist and with the flexibility of the mobile massage work, I decided to travel further and discover Asia. My husband and I had both been in employment where our times were dictated, so now we were enjoying the freedom that self-employment can give. Flying into Asia with no specific plans was fun, allowing life to unfold, following our intuition and travelling through Vietnam, Cambodia, Laos and Thailand having lifetime experiences with people, culture and beautiful asian elephants.

Everything in my life had seemed to work out with perfect synchronicity. Whilst in Asia, I had organised plenty of mobile massage events for my return to the UK and my therapy clients were booked in. Backpacking around Asia had given me the opportunity to put my mindset and meditation techniques into practise. It was fun to notice the flow and opportunities that appeared when I let go of trying to control everything and be more intuitive and open.

I had always wanted to go to Africa on a horse safari, but I could not see how this would be possible now, so using mindset techniques, I decided to take action and from a google search, I emailed two horse safari centres for volunteer positions and we were accepted by both. Sometimes things don't work out and we chose not to stay at the first South African venue. In life, it is important to have the discernment to say No when it isn't right for you.

The second safari centre in Botswana asked if I could teach their staff massage in return for a week's horse safari! How amazing, for me this was the perfect trade. My dream, a safari on horseback worth £3000 in return for teaching my skillset. When we landed in Botswana, it was everything I dreamed of being wild and free. We had amazing hosts and the staff brought joy to every moment dancing and singing as they went about their work.

The best part was the wild animals, a lioness on the track to the camp and meeting a herd of wild elephants when collecting the staff from their village in the mornings, one false move would cause them to charge. It was wild and real and you didn't take any chances. The guides had a sixth sense, they had great intuition and instincts. This was their world, their business and they knew their job.

This really taught me the importance of knowing your craft and being confident in its delivery, making a seamless, enjoyable experience for your clients. Every moment was changeable, and it was all about adapting to the moment.

At the camp, massaging clients under a tree in the shade, became interesting. With wild elephants arriving mid treatment and leopards leaving their kill in the branches above! Then the baboons stole the massage towels hanging them in the trees, and one night a hyena chewed through my saddle. I remember running from the bush toilet as an elephant ran down the embankment, ears flapping, trumpeting loudly. A calm, assertive mindset was required by all.

I was able to return to the safari centre the following year and continued to teach their staff about massage. By chance, I was there at the same time as two top equestrian event riders and a grand prix dressage rider, who were holding clinics for the owner and her staff. I was able to join in and receive top class training. A lifelong memory, jumping a cross country course out in the open bush having to watch out for elephants and lions.

In Botswana, I cheekily asked the Spanish Grand Prix dressage rider if I could spend some time at his dressage centre in Spain and learn more about this equestrian discipline. Dressage requires a real sense of connection, calm and presence. The mind-body connection is my business and horses are great teachers.

Meditation has helped me become much more aware in life and have the courage to take opportunities when they arise, as the saying goes, feel the fear and do it anyway.

I then invested in a beautiful treatment room and furthered my training in mindset and meditation, qualifying as a master mind calm and mind detox coach, going on to work within the Mind Detox Academy, mentoring students globally. I also overcame my fears in public speaking, seeking help and taking opportunities, where I have successfully given meditation presentations at events, festivals and in the workplace.

The Message

I believe that just because you can't see how something is possible, it doesn't mean that it can't happen, just keep taking action, be aware of, and explore the opportunities that present. I bought a house that wasn't currently for sale, in a coastal town that I'd never visited, and I transformed my business to travel with me. Unless you try, you'll never know if you can do something or enjoy it. Having my own business has had its ups and downs with huge learning curves, but it gives me freedom and choice. Everything I have done in the past has helped me become who I am today.Investing in a business coach to help me, I discovered that I enjoy writing, so now, sending regular calming newsletters to my subscribers, I also plan to write a book.Due to the pandemic and personal circumstances, I've experienced many lows, but that's ok. Through the sadness and stress has been enormous growth and my coaching business has benefited from moving online, where I now work with a global community. I love having a business that I am in charge of and that I can grow to serve the best needs of my clients. Learning is part of the adventure. Awareness is the key. I found opportunities come with being open and willing. Who knows who you will meet and what amazing things may happen when you take action.

"Your mind thinks it knows what it wants, but your soul knows the journey."
Follow your heart and enjoy the journey.
Success is a life that you love living.

BIO:

Josie Truelove is a Mindset and Calm Coach helping you to let go of anxiety, overthinking, fears and self doubt that are keeping you stuck in life. Working with Josie you will experience more calm, confidence and clarity in your life so that you can move forward with ease and achieve your hearts greatest desires, in your life, your relationships, work, health and hobbies.

www.josietruelove.com

9

WRITING TO HEAL

Mandy Dineley

A little sprinkling about me. I am passionate about encouraging people to express themselves at any special occasion and giving them the confidence to do so. I also love to create highly personalised wordy gifts for clients to give to loved ones.

I am fully committed to all my clients by giving them the chance to feel that they can say what they want to say in a true and heartfelt way. Specialising in wedding readings, bride's speeches, and wordy gifts. I love writing for all my clients, ensuring that they have the chance to thank or pay tribute to their loved ones, in such a gorgeous way.

Words really do add a unique blend of magic and emotion to any special occasion, making it highly personalised, it may sound strange, but I make people cry for the right reasons, by helping them find the right words, with the right emotion, and help them deliver a message in the most meaningful way.

I also write heartfelt and moving pieces for those sad occasions in life. I work with my clients in a gentle and empathetic way, to create a fitting tribute for their loved ones.

My qualifications for this are life, love, and loss and I use my singing, song writing skills to help my clients. Creating bespoke poetry and prose, creating those meaningful pieces, that make those special moments memorable.

Mandy Dineley, the 'wordy girl'.

The Day Everything Changed

I was on a beach in Puerto Pollensa, just a couple of days into our family holiday, looking at a prescription that I had just collected from a local Pharmacy. I had suffered a nasty allergic reaction to some sun cream. It was hot, sun cream was being applied to our three young children, we were looking forward to our day on the beach together.

My phone rang, it was a friend of my youngest brother, Russell from North Wales, she said "You know you said I could call you, if I ever needed you?" I replied, "Yes of course" and in that moment I thought, 'Oh my goodness, she wants me to go and collect Russell from Wales' an area he had moved to a couple of years previous. We had spoken recently about the need for Russell to see his family more, and of course, the family needing to see him, and I was happy to make that trip to see my brother. However, my thoughts were misplaced when the conversation turned incredibly sad. I was devastated to hear that Russell, our youngest sibling, our dark, shiny haired smiler, had passed away suddenly, at the age of 39.

I screamed out loud on the beach, it was too much for me to take in, our three young children looked at me, my husband came racing over, I just cried and cried in his arms. People were staring at me on that hot and sunny beach.

. . .

Before we go on

Writing has been a huge part of my life for many years. I started writing songs and poetry in my youth and now I write creatively for a living. I have been asked to write all sorts of things, from awkward wedding invitations to tributes to loved ones for both happy and sad occasions.

I started off my life as a vocalist in the north of England. The mainstay of the work were working men's clubs. They were tough crowds, but if you won them over, which we invariably did, they loved you, plus they had great pies and the money was good.

Years later, my husband was signed to a record company and touring with a band. We lived out in the sticks in Dippenhall, near Farnham, I spent a lot of time on my own, I bought myself an imperial 55 manual typewriter from a car boot sale and the pages just reeled off.

I have always found writing has healing powers, it's cathartic in a way that I had never fully appreciated, until I was given that devastating news.

The Hardest Decision

Going back to the sad moment on the beach when I was told that my brother had passed away. Once I composed myself, gathered a degree of control, I had to tell my Mum, I was the only one from our family who knew the situation. I went to our stiflingly hot car for privacy and made that dreaded call.

I said to my Mum that this is the saddest thing that I will ever have to tell you... I went on to tell her that Russell, her youngest child, who was just 39 years old, had died.

After I told my Mum about Russell, I had a difficult choice to make, should I stay in Spain, or head back to England to be with my parents and siblings? My heart was telling me one thing, but I wanted to stay with my husband and young children. My family in England told me to stay in Spain and try to make the most of the holiday. After all, it was a sudden death and there would have to be an autopsy, meaning the funeral would not take place for a few weeks. Nothing I could do would change the situation back home, and as I am one of six children, I knew that my parents would have the support they needed during this difficult time. So, after many tears and much soul searching, I decided to stay with my family on holiday in Spain. Not surprisingly there were numerous text and voice conversations with my parents' siblings and friends during the remaining days of our holiday.

Sadly, Mum and Dad have since passed away, grief has been a part of my life, but I really didn't want it to rule me, as I needed to be a happy Mum to our children, not a sad Mum 24 hours a day.

I recall one day during the last few days of our holiday we visited Old Pollensa town, the town has a beautiful chapel at the top, reached by 365 of the Calvari steps, all flanked by the most gorgeous Cypress trees. It was extra hot that day and under-standably, I was struggling to reach the top, but each step I took, our beautiful daughter Lily encouraged me by telling me "you can do it Mummy, come on, I know you can" She could sense my quiet struggle, tears were rolling down my face and Lily supported me all the way. I will never forget that moment.

When we eventually reached the top, the view was beautiful, and for some reason I just felt closer to my brother. We entered the tiny Calvario Chapel; it was beautiful. I said prayers and lit a candle for Russell and others that we had lost. It was a very spiritual moment; a moment that I just can't explain. The feeling and those moments were so intense and live with me today.

Looking back, it was a very difficult time. I felt lost, I was heartbroken, and I really needed to feel as though I could be useful and of help to others. Of course, I still had our family holiday to try and enjoy but I decided to put pen to paper, I started to write all my emotions down, my thoughts and feelings, trying in some way to compartmentalise 'things'. I had to be distracted, to be as present as I could be to my husband and children.

I always take notepads and pens with me, I wrote everything down that I could about Russell, I wrote down every text that I had from my heartbroken family, every text that I had from my brother's friend and my own friends. The phones weren't as sophisticated as they are these days, so I had to save the messages somehow, I had to save the emotions, it was a need that seemed to take over, as I felt far away from my family in the UK. I had to be a part of what the family were going through at home.

Writing kept me sane, it gave me a focus to help me get through the holiday, with at least some normality and amazingly enough, I did... We actually had a good holiday, of course, there were many moments when I broke down, but sunglasses helped a lot to hide my sadness and being a Mum, we are pretty good actors when we need to be, for the sake of our children.

Occasionally they saw me cry, as no emotion would have been a lie. As crazy as it sounds, I enjoyed the holiday, as I realised that I was fortunate to be there, that I had to live my life the very best I could for Russell, because Russell didn't have a choice and it was in that moment of clarity I realised that the one thing I wanted to do, was in my hands, my notebook and pen, my writing, my sharing of emotions, my encouragement for others to share how they felt and not to bottle feelings up.

Writing from that very moment, became a much bigger part of my life, bigger than I had imagined, I had been writing songs all my life, poems for free, but this took me to another level of creativity, it introduced me to a way that I could help others to heal, through trying to heal myself. I had no idea until that point that writing was as powerful as it was, that it could make a difference to myself and others.

My Beautiful Pen

My Beautiful Pen was gently borne from the grief I felt from losing my brother. I now have a greater sense that I should make the most of every single day and I owe this, in part, to my brother. We have a choice, but so sadly, he didn't.

I started my business with a few costs to get going, such as setting up my website, sorting a logo, signing up to some courses and I started writing personalised poems for special occasions such as weddings, milestone birthdays, anniversaries, eulogies, wordy gifts, blogs etc and all of this led to me to be commissioned to write a variety of things for all sorts of lovely clients, who wanted to give something precious and bespoke to a loved one, so my work became more varied and reactive, which as a creative, I love.

Setting up a business is not always easy, it is a time that support is often needed, such as business support, morale boosting and support from those who know you well, as it can be scary setting something up from scratch, as there is much to learn and taking that leap of faith can be a scary thing. I reached out to my networking groups, to my family, friends and so many were helpful with advice, support and importantly reassurance. I am so grateful to those who have faith in me, it really has and does make a difference.

All that I have worked on with my writing has enabled me to write with empathy and emotion for others, as I have been through a lot myself, I found the whole process each time that I wrote, heart wrenching, but also incredibly healing and uplifting, it helped me to get through those heart-breaking times, and this is how I started to write for other people for both happy and sad occasions.

My Beautiful Pen came out from a passion for writing. I had found the thing that I love the most and it was the thing that I needed to do, to help myself and others.

I called my writing business My Beautiful Pen because, for me, what is created from the pen is where the beauty lies, on the paper.

Words really are the key to our hearts...

BIO:

Mandy helps her clients to say what they want to say in a truly heartfelt way, gently capturing their thoughts, with her wonderful words, turning their feelings into personalised readings, with so much thought and attention to detail. The result is always a gorgeous surprise for the recipient, often creating happy tears.

Many of the pieces are read out at special occasions, Mandy gives her clients the confidence to stand up and read them out in front of friends and loved ones.

Each piece unique, creating the most memorable gifts that are just so personal and meaningful.

www.mybeautifulpen.uk

10

TRUST THE POWER OF YOUR VOICE

Laura Henshall

This is what the doctors said to my parents the evening I was born. "We're really sorry, but baby's born this early don't usually make it; if she does, there is a 75% chance that she will have a brain injury."

It was 1982, Manchester, UK, and it was raining. My mother had gone into labour for the third time in two weeks; she was 24 weeks pregnant. I was born weighing only 1lb 11oz, less than a kilogram. I had to fight for every breath and was attached to a ventilator for weeks. Thankfully, with an incredible team of doctors and nurses and many fighting spirits, I slowly got stronger day by day and was allowed to go home with my family three months later. I did make it with no brain injury or ongoing health issues.

I have always been on the petite side at 5ft 1, and those around me felt like they needed to protect me; that meant I relied on others a lot, and I was painfully shy. In hindsight, I can see how my story of being small and voiceless began.

I saw myself as 'tiny little Laura with a tiny little voice'. In addition, I attended a very strict C of E primary school, and any voice that may have been there was quietly buried for many years.

Have you ever wanted to speak up and say something, but the words just won't come out for some reason? I used to feel like that all the time, I could never seem to find the right words.

One of my favourite quotes is by Nelson Mandela:

"There is no passion to be found playing small, than settling for a life that is less than the one you are capable of living"

Before TNM Speakers Lab, I was playing small. I was in a job I didn't like, working as a Personal Assistant. I wasn't using my creativity or living my passion which at the time was to be an actress. I wanted to share important stories and go through the creative process of transformation. Being on stage was and still is my happy place, however, I dulled it down and continued to be who I thought I should be.

As luck would have it, I started working with Sydney acting coach Annie Swann. Annie is straight talking, highly intellectual and she observes and studies the human condition with finite detail. She knows how to tell a story with truth and depth. She shared her knowledge with me and she taught me what it takes to be a storyteller. She set me on my path to discover my confidence and use my knowledge for good in the world.

I thought to myself "How can I use my acting training and passion to help others? How can I build something that will support me and also serve others?".

Speakers Little Secret was born (now TNM Speakers Lab) because I am passionate and invested in each individual's voice. I want the people I work with to communicate with passion, excitement and without fear.

There is a rollercoaster of emotions that goes with running a business; the resistance to being seen, managing cash flow, getting clients, learning about online marketing, allowing myself to be heard, the list seems endless. When I first started, I had no idea what was ahead of me. Running my own business has taught me many things. One lesson that stands out for me, again and again, is that to grow and keep growing, we have to be consistent, have focus and take inspired action.

You see, it's all to do with where we put our energy. There is so much to running a business that we can direct our energy all over the place. Our speaking and communication skills cannot level up and bring in more money if we focus like a flashlight, not like a laser.

My speciality is speaking and communication; therefore, we will have some fun, focus, and find our voices in the following chapter. We will practise playing BIG so you can enjoy speaking to your clients and even, do that presentation, zoom call, TED talk, or fulfil your keynote dream.

I will go through three things with you that will help you with your business. :

- How to speak, so people listen
- Connecting to your authentic voice
- The power of storytelling

How to Speak, so People Listen

"The human voice. It's the instrument we all play. It's the most powerful sound in the world probably. It's the only one that can start a war or say, I love you. And yet, many people have the experience that when they speak, people don't listen to them. Why is that? How can we speak powerfully to make a change in the world?" - Julien Treasure

. . .

65

Have you ever had a situation where you are talking and the person you are talking to will interrupt, butt-in and talk over you? It's annoying, right? Maybe they'll start looking at their phone. Aside from being rude, there is a reason for this.

Your voice begins with your breath. With no breath, there is no sound. If you are not fully connected to your breath, you are not standing in your power.

If you are not standing in your power, it's more common to get interrupted, babble, ramble and go off on tangents. I know, I have been there. So what is the solution so our clients can hear our essential message?

- **Connect to your breath**. Connecting with your breath will bring you a myriad of benefits. The exercise I use most often is called box breathing or square breathing. Firstly, exhale and release the breath in your lungs. Slowly inhale for a count of four. Hold for a count of four. Exhale for a count of four. Be clear on your intention and continue to do this until you feel connected to your breath and ready to speak with intention.

- Talk slowly. The first thing I share with the people I work with is: **Slow down your speech.** Commonly, when we speak quickly without taking full breaths, we tell a story of nervousness and high energy. However, when we slow down even slightly, our brains can catch up with what we say.
- Consider are YOU really listening?

Listening is not the same thing as hearing. To share insights and valuable information for your customers and audience, you need to listen to their challenges so you can offer what they need.

Stellar Adler said," We must listen like animals in the forest."
I'd like you to go through your day today, breathe and listen
to each person you are talking to. Listen with your whole body,
not just your ears, and you will find that you become more
present.

Connecting to Your Authentic Voice

I believe we all have the capacity to have an expressive,
authentic voice, but what do we mean by authentic?

The London Speech workshop says authenticity is the
connection between what you are saying, how you are saying it,
and what you believe. I also think that this is where storytelling
and sharing our own experiences comes in. It allows us to be
truthful in what we are saying and for your customers and audience to see themselves in you.

The following question helped me consider what I was
putting out for my possible customers: How do you perceive
yourself and your place in the world?

At first, I saw myself as a newcomer who had a lot to learn.
Still, I also had evidence that I was determined, committed and
passionate about communication. I knew what my qualifications were, that I had run a theatre company with other actors,
and I also knew I could help others with my knowledge. My
authentic voice was able to come through as I had a level of
certainty about what I was saying, and I could also share what I
was still learning.

The Power of Storytelling

I adore storytelling, and I want you to use it in your business. Your talks and communication will be transformed into
an impactful experience for your audience. Learning how to
share stories in your business is the best investment you can

make. It is through emotion we connect and resonate with others.

Speaking and sharing your story and expertise through video and live public speaking is such a robust investment, and I want you to be able to have choices in your business.

Places where STORY works:
    Keynotes
    TED Talks
    Videos
    Website
    About page
    Sales pages
    Online Marketing Videos
    Emails to your subscribers
    Coaching packages
    Online programs
    Testimonials

Great questions to ask yourself are:

- How much of your story needs to go into everything you are doing across all platforms?
- How can I use different stories that will attract my ideal clients?
- What tense am I using?
- What is the most effective way to persuade, inspire and motivate my audience?
- What tone of voice am I using?
- Which platforms will I use to communicate my message?

Are you making the most of your 17,000 breaths each day? Is there something you need to say but have been procrastinating, resisting it for some reason? It takes courage to speak up and share your gifts, however, I promise you there are people out there waiting to hear from you. They need your expertise and knowledge so they can take their next steps.

What's next for TNM Speakers Lab?

My husband and I have merged our companies together. TNM Creative Media and TNM Speakers Lab. I have a bold vision to continue to support business owners and companies with their speaking skills and communication via online classes, in person events and workshops.

It's always been a dream of mine to build an acting and communication academy for children and young adults so we can support them in early development. We can create an environment where they feel safe to be themselves, speak up and revel in the magic of storytelling. Watch this space.

BIO:

Laura Henshall is an international speaker, actress and artist who leads workshops and seminars, giving people the support and encouragement they need to discover their true self-confidence and share it with the world.

She is the founder of TNM Speakers Lab and the creator of the online training program The Speakers Academy.

Laura guides us to connect with our confidence and turn our ideas and experiences into powerful TED-style talks, keynotes, and powerful videos through her work. Her work is holistic, playful and transformative. Her experience as a speaker and storyteller has seen her share her talks on stages in the UK, New York and Australia. She has gone on to support others to TEDx stages around the globe and grow their businesses through the medium of powerful speaking.

www.instagram.com/tnmspeakerslab

11

HANDSTANDS

Lisa Souter

There's something magical about doing handstands, that feeling of being upside down, the way you have to control every part of your body, the slightest movement to your centre of mass and gravity takes over, or perhaps it's the control you yield over your body, the competition with yourself to be upside down, that sense of personal achievement... for no one else can do your handstand... you have to work at it. Even now you'll find me sneaking in a handstand somewhere, in front of a Christmas tree, at the beach, hotel lobby, at the airport, for once a gymnast always a gymnast, that bug never leaves you, and it brings such joy.

As a child I was always upside down, I remember my dad constructed a climbing frame out of scaffold poles, it had monkey swings and I'd be outside for hours swinging and hanging upside down.

My love of gymnastic coaching started at 13yrs, I could proudly say "I taught them that", by 15yrs I was the club's youngest assistant coach. I'd been coached by some inspiring people and competed abroad. I remember thinking how lucky I was and how wonderful it must be to give this experience to others, but in the 1980's, you couldn't be a full-time gymnastic coach, that just wasn't a proper job!

I learnt so much at gymnastics, life skills I wouldn't truly understand till many years later but as a child I always knew I'd own my own business someday.

Fast forward, I've graduated university, working full time in the House Building Industry, the TA (Territorial Army) and as a volunteer coach. I loved the diversity. Corporate life was a mix bag of old-meets-new, resistance to change and collaboration on projects. Military training showed me how different men and women worked, to play to each other's strengths, the importance of non-emotional reflection, and how to embrace challenges working together as a team. Gymnastics gave me freedom to dream. Over the years the number of times I've said to myself, you can do this, you're a gymnast, you can do anything you set your mind to. So, I did!

Everything in life is a character-building moment, the people we meet, the friends we make, the hurt we feel, the joy we share, it helps develop and shape our character. People come, people go, we learn from them if we choose to and doors open and close all around us. Sometimes we're too scared to step through into the unknown, another time we're pushed through, with resistance high, but later thankful for the shove! Our characters never stop developing, evolving, we just get a little more set in our ways.

That A-ha moment...

...Came whilst listening to a talk about a new form of gymnastics, TeamGym, starting up in the UK.

Within a week I had a TeamGym class, responsible for 24 gymnasts, 2 coaches and 7 weeks later, I took a team to compete at the British TeamGym Championships. The aim being inspiration and experiencing a life changing moment. Looking back, that was one hell of an achievement. Aside from teaching, co-ordinating the gymnastics, I learnt the rules, communicated with parents, ordered competition kits, arranged transport, overnight accommodation, restaurants and team travel. We made friends, created memories and went away wanting more.

We competed at the British TeamGym Championships in 1997, 1998, 1999, 2000 alongside other regional competitions in the South. Competitions took place around the country in places like Dewsbury, Nottingham, Newcastle, Aldershot, London and for some gymnasts they had never left Southampton and here they were travelling further than some of their parents had travelled in a lifetime.

By 2000 my teams had outgrown the club I was at, our "Why's" were no longer aligned and not wanting to let the gymnasts down I started Horizon TeamGym. Most of the gymnasts followed. I was still working full time at this point.

Horizon was started to continue giving back life experiences, whilst being completely self-sufficient and helping towards competition expenses, it was a vehicle to make dreams happen. Having a business like this, supporting continuous learning and giving pleasure to your soul and others, is priceless.

Over the next 21 years...

Horizon TeamGym competed / attended local, regional, national and European events, travelling right across the UK from Dundee to Poole, Belgium, Italy, Iceland and Denmark, making friends wherever we went and inspiring generations of gymnasts. All those accolades, achievements over the years didn't come without adversity, there were countless times I'd been close to giving up, but somehow found the strength to keep on putting one foot in front of the other and keep moving forwards.

I've judged Nationally since 1999 and as a European Brevet Judge since 2001. I've travelled to various European countries judging, yet it took till 2014 to judge at the European TeamGym Championships, Iceland, that's 13yrs to achieve that dream, and yes, I still get that uncontrollable excitement at competitions, goosebumps with amazing performances and just love watching the progress these incredible athletes and coaches achieve year on year, always pushing the sporting boundaries to the next level.

In 2004 I was made redundant from the corporate world and by 2005 had opened up Horizon's first satellite centre. We started with 2 classes on 1day and quickly grew to 2days, 5 classes plus competitive squad training. I was managing a growing gym club and coaching, all with my 2yr old in tow.

Horizon's 2009 TeamGym camp took us to Italy with another club. We all returned inspired and by 2010 collaborated to form Synergy. We produced a new Senior Mixed Team that both qualified 2nd and ranked 2nd at the British TeamGym Championships. This collaboration inspired a new generation of young adults and coaches. It came with learning many lessons, ending with some big personal goals.

1. I wanted to start a new business
2. To get my Level 5 HPC (High Performance Coach) qualification
3. Give Horizon gymnasts the opportunity to train for a European Championship

In Sept 2012 I opened up my preschool business Woodland Owls Ltd. It's funny how looking back at the thought process, business planning couldn't have been more different compared to Horizon. In the Early Years sector, I could emotionally detach myself, staff were employed to do a job which meant I could focus on the business.

In 2012 I passed my L5 HPC qualification after 50hrs of mentored coaching with an IPC (International Performance Coach), a trip to Iceland with my team to train with their coaches. I became 1 of 9 HPC TeamGym coaches in GB.

In 2011 an experiment, trialling gymnasts from multiple clubs, resulted in the main lead coach and co-ordinator withdrawing just a few months into the project with the choreographer reducing commitment. 22 gymnasts (15-27yr olds), including 3 Horizon, were now on the verge of having their European dream destroyed. Together with 2 coaching friends Janet Allabush and Claire Wright, we agreed to support the team's journey, this was a voluntary 18mth training commitment. To this day it still amazes me what we went through to make this happen.

Infinity performed on the TV game show "Let's get Gold" playing for £100,000, their routine encompassed all that is TeamGym. They made it through to the final but didn't win. The whole ITV exposure was incredible, they became famous and I facilitated venue hire, equipment usage for rehearsals and filming. At the Fountain Studios, London they had their own team stylist, who fitted them out with costumes, hair and makeup.

Infinity won the Senior Mixed Team Southern TeamGym Qualifiers and became the British TeamGym Champions 2012, then competed at the European TeamGym Championships in Denmark coming 6th in the finals. It was a bucket full of firsts for many team members and nail biting right to the end. Two Horizon gymnasts made it to the finals.

Then in 2014 another Horizon gymnast competed at the Europeans. I just burst with pride when I think of their achievements.

Horizon was growing...

In 2017 I recruited admin help. I had 14 coaches, was sinking fast in a sea of admin and we opened our 2nd satellite centre.

Splitting my time between the 2 businesses was challenging enough and a new cycle emerged, as I focused on 1 business it thrived and the other started a downward trend then I'd swap attention, that business would thrive and the other started a downward trend. It was very frustrating. It took 7years to recruit the right staffing team for Woodland Owls. In that time the staff turnaround was huge. Each recruitment was costly and government funding was starting to be stripped right back. That coupled with increases in hall hire, minimum wage, pension and NI contributions, I was looking at serious trouble in just a few years.

That's when I joined Hampshire Women's Business.

There are so many benefits to running your own business. Freedom, diversity, direction, but I found myself working in excess of 60hrs weekly. The bigger I grew the more resistance I encountered.

Then adversity struck, in 2018 my 2 main coaches left. The hole they left behind and the crumbling structure with gymnasts leaving to follow them or go elsewhere was nothing compared to the broken trust I felt inside.

My 2nd centre closed leaving a huge debt and nearly took me down with it. Should I give up?

I picked myself back up and diversified...

In 2019 I took on a dance teacher, a rhythmic gymnastics centre and a L3 TeamGym coach.

I could actually see the tide turning. We were going to be ok. Then Covid struck!

I still find it hard to believe the way Covid, which started Dec 2019 in Wuhan, China, sent the World into spiralling lockdowns. My preschool business stayed open for key worker families but ultimately couldn't sustain the financial loss, I couldn't furlough staff and, upsettingly, the doors closed Jul 2020.

Horizon moved to online zoom training, with a determination to stay open. During 2020-21 we stopped / started with physical and zoom training, it took 14months to reopen 1 centre. I lost 6 coaches, suspended one training day, lost another 2, a fall in numbers, staff shortages, Covid, mental health all being contributing factors.

I've not stopped. I've pivoted, supported, adapted, found solutions and not given up. I've led a team of coaches through anxiety and embraced change. I've moved to online platforms for invoicing, accounts, legalised T&C's, launched a new website, started Horizon Fitness Online and rebranded to Horizon Gymnastics.

So, what does the future hold?

To look forward you must first look back, reflecting over the last 21 years I can recall so many stories.

I've nurtured shy children into confidence, shown angry children how to lead, and taught adults how to coach challenging children.

At Horizon we achieve dreams. Some past gymnasts have stayed within the leisure industry, running their own businesses whilst others have studied medicine, become doctors or physiotherapists, joined the entertainment industry, continued their passion for coaching, education, became engineers, joined the services, but they all took away that knowledge that anything is possible, don't ever give up.

The ripple effect outwards from Horizon are far reaching and still rippling. This is the legacy Horizon leaves behind and who is Horizon, well it's Lisa Souter and a collection of amazing people who have travelled along this path with me.

So, what's next?

Well for now it's regrouping after Covid, supporting the growth of Rhythmic, rolling out the Young Leadership Academy and always making time for handstands!

BIO:

Married since 2002 to an amazing, understanding husband, a life partner since 1990, Lisa Souter is a mum to 2 boys and founding Director of Horizon Gymnastics.

A coach since 1985, she believes that every gymnast and coach should be at the centre of their learning development. She is a TeamGym judging tutor, assessor and coaching mentor. Travelling throughout the UK and Europe for judging commitments.

www.horizon-gymnastics.co.uk

BOUNCE BACK STRONGER

Angie Brown

January 2015, I was being made redundant for the first time, and from a job I LOVED. Although it was a shock to the system, I knew it was happening and had been preparing for it. When the day finally came, the reality of it hits you in the face, and knocks you straight onto your butt! Well, that's what happens when two large companies collide. It makes sense not to have duplicate roles but to merge them; after all, that's what a merger is right? Still a shock to be out of work but great to have funds to lean on after 12 years of service.I was looking forward to putting my feet up, spending some time with my son and being a full-time Mum. Truth is, although I loved it and could do what I wanted, when I wanted, I was bored. Doing nothing is boring and it made me feel lazy. I was thinking perhaps I could go it alone and start up my own business, but heck, where do you start with all that malarkey? What would I do? I had been an Executive Assistant working alongside senior leaders, compiling reports, working with project management teams, coordinating management teams and meetings, working on processes and procedures etc. etc. Always in the back office, not the one that stood up front delivering. No, I was in the engine room.Whilst I was thinking about my next step, my confidence saboteur turned up and told me I could not go it alone and I was crazy to think I could. *What makes you think you can run a business? Who do you think you are? No one is going to want what you offer. Get over yourself!* Jeez, what a bummer that was. I was scared to try. Instead, I picked myself up and dusted myself down and reluctantly sought another corporate role hoping and praying it would be very much like the brilliant role I had been made redundant from.

I accepted a job working with several Vice Presidents and the Managing Director – they were so great to work with, but as with all things, there were changes made and I ended up completely regretting that move. The people I started the role with were replaced, and that is all I am saying about that! It did make me realise that there was so much more I could give and instead of supporting one or two people, in a company, I could support many business owners.

I took the plunge, and I started a virtual assistant (VA) business in July 2016, working part-time initially. I ignored the nagging from my saboteur and just got on with it. It was really scary. I had no idea what I was doing or how I was going to get any clients or pay the bills, but I did it nonetheless. I took that step, bought equipment and software licences and was ready to go. Go where though...what did I need to do. Google can be your friend so I looked up networking and chose a local group to visit.

It was so hard walking into that first networking meeting and not knowing a single person. Luckily, I was greeted by a lovely lady who looked after me. When asked, I did my pitch with a bright red embarrassed face and thought, *jeez thank goodness that is over!* I went back many more times and started to learn about how to work the room ethically. There was none of that *here's what I do, buy it now,* it was more along the lines of getting to know everyone and chatting, asking and answering questions. That was the best bit and I am good at that. To this day, I still don't like the pitchy stuff, I guess that is the introvert in me.

I ran my VA business for a few years and knew it would not be my final role. You see, I started my career as an Office Junior and worked all through the ranks to an Executive Assistant role and loved all that I did. But, for me, being a VA felt like a step back. I am not dissing anyone who is a VA as it is a valuable role and one I am grateful for having had, but I knew it wasn't what I truly wanted to do. It seems that fate helped with that.

In 2020, COVID-19 hit, turning the world upside down. A majority of my clients pulled work back and took it in-house. I could understand why, they were not sure what was happening to them either or where their next payment was coming from. The future, for everyone, was proper scary. You could find me rocking in the corner with my head in my hands as I honestly had no clue when I would get paid again. No one had any idea how long this situation was going to go on for. One thing I did know, I had to do something about my situation.

A friend set up a pro-bono group of coaches. They offered 6 weeks of support with one of their coaches. What a gift that was! I took up the offer feeling so grateful for the chance. In one of the meetings, I was asked *What do you truly love to do?* It was part of my assignment, and I wrote reams of things down, getting it all out there and visible was such a great thing to do. There's nothing better than a good brain dump for sorting things out. It helped tremendously.

I love helping people and I am always volunteering (Chair of the PTA, school invigilator, COVID-19 helpline support). I love teaching too and when I started writing about that, the passion flew out of me. I particularly love it when I see the transformation of the people I work with. From frustrated to flying. From swamped to swimming. When you see that lightbulb go on when someone properly *gets it*, it is one of the best feelings in the world.

I started teaching Canva. For those that have not heard of it, it is software that allows you to create graphics for social media, brochures, logos, business proposals, e-books, video books and so on and so on – the list is long! It is an essential tool to have in your business.

As you may have ascertained, I am pretty passionate about it. I created several courses which started with 8-week interactive programmes followed by 5-day courses helping beginners and intermediates. It was the best feeling.

Around the time of the pro-bono coaching, I was meeting up with business friends every Monday lunchtime on Zoom. We would encourage each other, listen and pick each other up. Give guidance and simply be there for each other. I cannot tell you how empowering and life-changing that was for me and still is to this day. From that came so much more and my business is still evolving. I learnt not to be afraid of what was coming next. I started putting out short "how to" videos on all kinds of topics and getting such brilliant feedback – it is so encouraging.

I felt more confident and was evolving my business to something I loved doing. It's incredible how making tweaks to things and listening to yourself and suggestions from others can give you the focus and determination to get to the next stage. I was on the right track.

Life is brilliant, isn't it? There are days when you feel desperate and wonder what the heck is going to knock you off your feet again and why me? And then there are the days when you bounce back up with your rubber arse and get on with it. When, what appears to be bad things happening, have you noticed how good things appear straight after?

I was looking back at my corporate history. At those tasks that had to be done in a certain way. Remembering the '*Office*

Bible' that would be put together for when you were off sick or on your holidays, allowing temporary staff to take over for you. It occurred to me, *why can't you have this in an online business?* Well…why not? When you are sick, who is going to take over for you? When you are on holiday, are you taking your laptop? What does your family think about that? When do you get to switch off?

Many clients said that time is an issue for them. *There are not enough hours in the day. I don't have time to show someone how to do what I do. I don't have enough time to spend with my family. I can't bring on new clients as I don't have time. They won't do the tasks the same way as I do.* I run time management courses with 6 modules and including outsourcing. You don't have to employ someone through payroll, you can outsource to service providers such as VA's, bookkeepers, marketing specialists. It doesn't cost as much as you think either.

Why don't you calculate how much a task you currently do, costs you? Look at your hourly rate and how long it takes you. Then look at the average cost per hour to outsource to a professional. You will be surprised how much money and time it would save you. Hiring someone to do those tasks, which they probably do daily for their other clients, you know they will be so much faster and more efficient than you.

With your business processes and standard operating procedures in place, you could guarantee a task would be completed the way you want. Now, here's a thought, what if they have a smarter and more efficient way of doing it? Be open to listening to their expertise and re-write your procedures if their suggestion is worth adopting.

Hiring someone can be daunting but give it a try. Agree to do a trial and book 5 or 10 hours with them as a starting point. Be clear with your instructions and ask them to repeat back what they understand the task to be – this is crucial as you will learn a lot about yourself and them too.

It took me over a year to transition from VA to Business Management Consultant. This year will see more change as I launch a membership to help online business owners move forward and expand their businesses. I do believe that for your business to grow, you do need certain things in place, and that is why I created my Business Nuts and Bolts Facebook group.

I am an empathic introvert, a Reiki Master with an affinity with soul centred creatives. I love to surround myself with people who have a positive perspective and are accountable for what is happening to them in their lives.

I've created a safe place for those who are not sure what their next steps are. Allowing them to express what they are hoping to achieve in their business. Not to fear expanding. Allowing them to learn systems and processes that will build the best foundations for business growth. Giving them support and belief they can achieve their business goals, wishes and dreams. Perfect for new business owners and those wanting to expand.

I love what I do.

BIO:

After over 30 years working in large corporate companies, Angie set up her own business in July 2016 to help support other solo online business owners. She is passionate about finding the solutions to grow a smarter business and is driven by successfully achieving goals. Angie is skilled in listening and understanding the needs of her clients and can give clients their most valued commodity…TIME

Angie knows that change is inevitable and necessary for businesses and organisations to survive and thrive.

https://www.facebook.com/groups/businessnutsandbolts/

13

COME ON A HELICOPTER RIDE
WITH ME!

Jo James

Ooh, are you looking to set up your own business now? How exciting, come over to the bright side! There are so many people ready to help you adapt and create the business and lifestyle you *really* want now.

You probably have some ideas already, so it's time to make some changes and put them into action. As my coach said to me once, "if not now, when?"

I've worked through 3 recessions but never a pandemic before! But I have created new services, moved country, and now go to art classes. Something I really wanted to do but never had the time for.

Being able to slow down to speed up has been quite a different experience as the whole world changed. But here we go! I've learned it's best to embrace change. To find joy in the journey and you'll love building your business.

It's such a ride!

Hello, I'm Jo James, with over 25 years hands-on experience of growing 6 and 7 figure businesses starting with developing pubs and restaurants in my twenties.

Running my own businesses has been challenging, rewarding, frustrating and so wonderful too. It's been a roller coaster of a ride! I love helping people realise their potential and to take action to change their situation for the better.

Change is a constant thing in life, we can rely on things changing. I've personally changed course every 7 years making significant changes to how I live and work.

When I was 23, I managed my first pub called The Canonbury Tavern in Islington. At first it was taking only £1500 a week, but in only nine months time I grew it to £15,000 a week, £750,000 per year. That's 10 times business growth! I was hooked.

I stayed there for two years and with a massive bonus from my efforts, took a year off and went round the world. I love meeting new people and immersing myself into new cultures, eating new foods, and exploring our beautiful world. It was an amazing experience I will never forget, and I learned so much along the way.

When I returned to the UK, I called my Area Manager and told him I was back! Next stop, Barnstaple in North Devon to take over a 13th Century Coaching Inn, with a 50-seater restaurant. They knew how to tempt me! I grew profits and doubled turnover in 12 months to £1.2 million, but then had to make a big life change.

Business was great, but my relationship had changed and I left my first husband when I was 28, went to London by myself and managed a retail health store. But boy I needed more money and a car!

After a year learning all about vitamins and helping people improve their health, I joined a leading food brand as an Area

Sales Manager, and grew my area to 7- figures, from selling over the phone and face to face meetings to schools, restaurants and Wembley Stadium!

Turning 30, I needed another new challenge, so started afresh as a Permanent Consultant for a high street recruitment agency. Wow, I loved it! Working through the first dot com boom, a recession and then seeing in the new century I was asked to be a Manager. But after filling out far too many excel spreadsheets for Head Office, I knew it was time for me to step up, take that leap and start my own business.

I really wanted to help my candidates to develop their careers, so at 35, I started my own Recruitment Business specialising in Media and Medical Health. I successfully ran this London based business for 12 years, starting on the dining room table with a laptop and a phone.

Working in London taught me how you've got to stand out, have structure and processes in place, be consistent with your sales and marketing, and deliver excellence. Excellence you can achieve, don't even think about perfection!

Then I lost nearly everything

Business was great, we had a great team and we were about to move into a three-storey office when the financial crash happened. I lost 75% of my business in 3 weeks. It was a horrible time. But again these massive changes led to greater things.

When networking in London, and chatting to other business owners, I noticed so many were oozing talents and skills, they were great at what they did but not earning the money they thought they would when they started out on their own. They were getting stressed with how to find new clients to work with and overwhelmed with having just been made redundant, or losing big clients.

I hate seeing people not doing what they want to or feeling trapped or stuck and I didn't want them to have to go back to their old job or way of life. This all led me to create AmberLife in 2009 – to empower women to take action on their goals, give them a confidence boost to create a profitable business, and be independent.

I share with them my strategies on how to sell their services and products effectively, enabling them to grow their business. Yes, 'sales' maybe something you may first shy away from, but learning these skills are *vital* to your success.

I call it sales, the Anti-selling way!

I delivered my first AmberLife Sales Training in 2010 and loved it! I could see the group having brilliant 'a-ha' moments, overcoming their fears throughout the day and getting great results. One attendee, a creative designer earned £10,000 in 10 days following the training, and another earned an EXTRA £130,000 in 10 months. Brilliant results, I was like a very proud Aunty.

So it was decided! I wound down my recruitment agency and created AmberLife, to help small business owners *stay* in business and *grow* their business, and importantly, feel good along the way.

Since 2009, I have helped hundreds of creative business owners, executives, consultants and coaches, get clear on what to focus on and with my sales tips and techniques, they can convert those leads into clients – the ideal clients they *want* to work with.

As well as focusing on sales and marketing, I incorporate the brilliant NLP skills I've learned and honed over the years, because it works.

Neurolinguistic Programming (NLP) explores how people think, feel and act to perform effectively. It's THE best self-development tool I have discovered, and is widely used in health, education, business and sports worldwide, because 'it gets the results you want'.

Many of my clients *double* (or triple) their revenue and increase profits when working with me. I'm super proud of the results my clients gain and love seeing them step up and grow in confidence as they achieve their goals.

What goals do you have? What do you want to achieve next?

Let's 10 X your results.

To help you get started, enjoy a Helicopter ride with me to THINK BIG.

Once you have treated yourself to the ride, you will be able to see where best to put your focus and energies to help you make the revenue you want to.

So, prepare for take-off.

Come on a helicopter ride with me!

This is one of THE most **powerful 6 step visualisation exercises to get your creative juices flowing.** Relax. See what you discover.

Ready?

Good.

Now, enjoy the ride!

1 . Write down the financial target you want for the next 3 months, Q1.

Maybe you've written a target of £5,000 or £20,000, whatever works for you. Remember to multiply by 4 to get your annual revenue.

2 . Now, add a zero to the quarterly target, so as in this example, it will now be £50,000 or £200,000.

Hmm, I bet that feels more exhilarating, doesn't it? You

might well be thinking, what do you need to do *differently* to achieve your new boosted goal?

So now imagine...

3 . Stepping inside your virtual helicopter, fasten your seat belt, and let's go for a ride and *think big to get ideas* on how you can *achieve* your new boosted goal.

You may want to read through this exercise first, then come back to this point, close your eyes and let your imagination do the work for you.

4 . Imagine flying high above your desk and as you ascend higher, past the roof of your house, higher so you can see an area much wider below you. Rise again and see the land, your country, and more, as a bird sees it. Fly higher so you get that aerial view.

5 . Let the power of your imagination help you to see where it's taking you. With your new financial target in mind, get creative on how you're going to achieve that.

6 . Looking out of the helicopter window, what can you see yourself doing? Are you online talking to camera to your desired audience across the globe? Going live on socials? Working differently?

Who are you talking to? Where are you networking to meet more people?

And one of my favourite questions...

What have you just thought of that might sound like a crazy idea at first, but is probably the thing that will get you there?

Where are you going?

Are you collaborating, joining forces with someone?

Writing a book? Creating a new service?

What are you doing differently?

Write down your ideas as they appear to you.

You might have just seen a brilliant idea before your very eyes as to ways and new avenues that you can take.

When you are ready, come down to earth gently and sit back into your seat in your office or wherever you started from feeling refreshed, revitalised and raring to go!

Excellent. From completing the Helicopter Ride exercise you now have new ideas on how to generate revenue and build your business this year.

We all need support.

Being the owner of your business gets lonely at times too, so seek out help and be with other business owners. Look into working with a coach, join a mastermind group and go networking! Having like-minded people around you will speed up your success and it's much more fun! I have met the most kind, inspiring, brilliant business owners.

Networking events are online now as well as face to face, a wonderful upside from the pandemic. You can grow your business and create a global network, all from the comfort of your home.

My events are called Contacts and Cocktails which I was able to adapt online to give everyone support. Cocktails can be delivered to your door and the networking is facilitated so everyone gets to know you and your expertise. Recently we celebrated 7 years of networking together, here's to the next 7!

What's next?

I'm excited about what's going to happen next. During the pandemic I relocated to Portugal and changed my life again. Moving to Portugal was one of our long-term dreams so we bought a villa a few years ago, and recently decided to move here full time.

Coaching online works very well and soon, covid permitting, I will be hosting retreats here in the Algarve, Portugal and providing my new services called Strategies in the Sun. A goal I've had for about 4 years now!

So whether your goals are short term or long term, take action on your dreams and celebrate along the way. Every step counts.

And remembering your journey and insights from your Helicopter ride, what's the next step you can take right now to help you realise your new boosted goal?

Go for it! I'm cheering you on from here.

Embrace the changes and opportunities ahead and enjoy building your business and creating the lifestyle you desire.

To your success and happiness,

BIO:

Jo James: Business Coach, Sales Trainer and Author of Make Your Mondays Matter. Join my newsletter for proven business growth tips and a mindset boost.

www.amberlife.com

14

FROM SHY TO SEEN

Caroline Joynson

I guess my story *really* begins when my role was made
redundant from my 'dream job' when I was pregnant with
my second daughter.

Until this point I had very much followed the traditional
path – from school to university (via an amazing gap year in
Australia), from marriage to motherhood. I chose business
studies as the most likely subject to result in a job and studied it
to degree level. To me, success was all about having a good job
and the security that came with it.

At this point I was only vaguely aware of public relations
(PR), it was a degree course we tended to sneer at – full of 'PR
girls' – confident, glamourous and cocky. I'd never heard of PR
when I applied for my degree, and certainly had no intention of
ever working in PR, I wasn't that kind of girl.

Looking back at my preconceptions I'm pretty sure these
stemmed from being painfully shy as a child. I couldn't order
my own food in a restaurant and my dream job was to be a
librarian, so I wouldn't have to talk to anyone. I also had the

belief that good girls don't 'show off' or blow their own trumpet. How wrong I was.

HR to PR

I was ecstatic when I landed my one-year work placement in HR at corporate giant BT. It was my dream gig, or so I thought. Whilst there, it was announced via the news that 2,500 BT managers were being made redundant, and I realised I didn't want to be part of a department handling that. And that's when I started to look for other options. I discovered that with my love of writing and photography, along with a healthy interest in business, PR made perfect sense for me.

Returning to university for my final year, I was told by a careers officer that "Everyone wants to get into PR, it's very competitive you know". This made me more determined than ever, a quality that has served me well in my chosen profession; one where coverage isn't guaranteed and you have to take a lot of 'no's' before you get a 'yes'. My PR career began straight out of university with a role in a small agency. Put that in your pipe and smoke it careers officer! And same to you, shy girl who wanted to be a librarian!

I quickly learnt that PR is hard graft. A profession synonymous with pitching to journalists and essentially 'selling' client stories. Where you have three bosses – the client, your manager, the media. A role where you are reacting to the news agenda as well as trying to create and influence it.

Moving to a bigger agency, I worked on a succession of perception-smashing campaigns – from launching the national recycling campaign to promoting international matches for the England women's football team. The power of PR to influence behaviour and challenge accepted norms was something I relished, and still do.

From there I went in-house to become the Senior Press

Officer at a national museum. I thought I'd made it, my dream job, but, a bit like the work placement, it wasn't what I expected. The work was interesting and exciting – promoting international film festivals and photography exhibitions – but the organisational culture was challenging to say the least.

Having battled for flexible working after my first maternity leave, I was preparing for my second when I got the email saying a change was being made to the team – but only to my role. And so we're back at the real start of my story.

Redundancy to freelancer

My redundancy. I was devastated, humiliated, rejected. I felt like the world could see that I wasn't good enough. My core belief of needing a good job to be successful and secure lay in tatters. I couldn't even tell my parents over the phone and drove over an hour to tell them in person. But it was the best thing that could have happened to me.

It gave me my freedom, it gave me the chance to rebuild my confidence, to build a business around my husband and two young daughters, on my own terms. Of course, it was daunting. I'd only ever worked for other people. I'd always had a boss and been part of a team. But I'd managed to stand on my own two feet during my first maternity leave, so I could definitely do it again.

I'd suffered with post-natal depression during my first maternity leave, and now faced it for a second time. It was brutal but I recovered. When my second daughter was 11 months old I was offered the opportunity to take on some free-lance clients. I initially turned down the opportunity, having lost my confidence, but realising I had nothing to lose gave me the opportunity to give it a try. I've never looked back. Recovering from post-natal depression gave me the belief that if I could come back from being so unwell, I could do anything, and that belief has stayed with me ever since.

Freelancing allowed me to become my own boss, doing PR my way and with great success – I was consistently fully booked with clients. This was down to my existing network of contacts, along with LinkedIn. I didn't even have a website. Working with owner-managed, passion-led businesses doing amazing things reignited my love for PR and its power to get more good stories out into the world.

However, there was only me in the business and I was purely trading time for money. I was up to capacity and struggling to balance client work with the demands of a young family. There had to be another way.

Making the move online

Towards the end of 2016 I became aware of Carrie Green, founder of the Female Entrepreneur Association. She was about to publish her first book and built a Facebook community around it. For the first time I was surrounded by other women with their own businesses and started to see the potential of building an online business.

In September 2017, my youngest daughter started school and I had five days a week on my hands. Finding myself quite lonely in business at this point I teamed up with two other local women with their own businesses to launch our own local women's networking group. It's one of my proudest achievements. This was my first experience of building an online (and offline) community. I also started working from a co-working space around this time, I realised working at home on my own every day was not good for my mental health.

I started to really focus on how I could leverage my time and expertise by teaching groups of business owners how to do their own PR rather than purely doing it for them. I developed a series of workshops which I tested with local business owners and realised I could make a business out of teaching people how to blow their own trumpets!

I could see clear patterns with my new clients – solo business owners who had turned their passion into a business. They weren't clear on who they were trying to reach or what they wanted to achieve. They were so busy working in the business that they were overwhelmed with their communications. They didn't understand the power of their story and expertise, let alone how to harness it to build relationships with their audience.

I realised I could help them by taking them through my PR planning process – and my PR Strategy Session service was born. I held my first Strategy Session in January 2019 and have since gone on to deliver multiple sessions each year.

Around this time, I invested in coaches, courses and a mastermind. I was going all-in – but I still had a full roster of 'done for you' clients. I was essentially trying to run two business models at the same time and have been ever since. Not something I'd recommend – if you can go all-in on one business model, do!

Building a brand

I was ready to establish my own brand. I'd come up with the name Cheerleader PR and was trying to decide if I was brave enough to use it. It felt big and scary to start my own brand, I'd only ever used my own name before (and no one could spell it!).

For me, being someone's cheerleader in business is about championing them and sharing their good news and stories. It's what I've always done. But business owners need to be able to do this for themselves, and this is where I could help. I could teach them to become their own best cheerleader.

I launched my website in June 2019, along with two in-person PR workshops. I also hosted my first online workshop which proved to me that I could offer PR training online, geography was no longer a barrier. I've since gone on to offer 1:1 PR mentoring as well as group programmes.

Getting visible

To make it in the online world, I had to go from being 'behind the scenes' and championing my clients to promoting myself. It was time to get visible and people often ask me how I've managed to do this, especially when they know that I was so shy as a child.

My answer is through being consistent when it comes to communications and through trial and error when it comes to the tech. I practiced going live in other people's Facebook groups well before I started my own. I went live in my Facebook group every week and sent out a weekly email to my mailing list. I blog every other week and deliver guest expert sessions in other people's groups on a regular basis. I've guested on podcasts and, not surprisingly, I've been featured by the media on multiple occasions.

I find sharing my story and expertise easy – that's at the heart of PR after all – but I find the sales side more challenging. PR is about encouraging action through building a compelling case. Rarely do you ask outright for the 'sale'. But it's something I am working on. After all, my motto in PR is 'you don't ask, you don't get' and the same is true with sales. It's just finding the right way for me.

Championing a better world

I entered 2020 ready to take Cheerleader PR to the next level. Then Covid hit. The world as I knew it turned on its head and I was desperate to do something to help with the relief effort.

I had worked with The Real Junk Food Project before and they were mobilising their network to get surplus food to those who needed it. I offered to manage their PR and threw myself into promoting their amazing work. They managed to redistribute over one million meals to those who needed them during the UK lockdowns.

What the future holds

The pandemic, and working with TRJFP, changed me – or maybe it reignited my passion to champion ordinary people doing extraordinary things. From the founder of TRJFP, to the England's women's football team, to making recycling mainstream; I love championing people, campaigns and causes that are changing the world for the better. This is where the future of Cheerleader PR lies.

It's time to write my next chapter.

BIO:

Caroline Joynson is a PR Strategist and the founder of Cheerleader PR. Caroline's mission is to empower passionate business owners to promote themselves with confidence - helping them to gain media coverage and PR so they can raise their profile, build relationships and make more sales. With 20 years' PR experience, Caroline offers PR mentoring, courses and consultancy. She works with clients locally, nationally and internationally, helping them to get clear on their message and share it alongside their unique story and expertise.

www.cheerleaderpr.com

15

LOOK, MUM, NO HANDS!

Rachael Welford

People talk about what a business takes from you; how it's hard and relentless; never having a day off; living for your clients. My experience has been different. Running my business changed me for the better.

Having overcome major traumas, depression, anxiety and PTSD, my business gave me purpose. Do I get excited about invoicing and emails? Not really. But I do get enthusiastic about the impact my work has on the world.

Let's go back to the beginning... I haven't always dreamed of having a business. I had a successful career in action sports and loved it. I travelled the world snowboarding and met some incredible people. I shared rooms with Ronnie Wood, Blondie and Meat Loaf, and even blagged The Libertines into an after-party by pretending to be their PR. I had grown up in the time of ladette culture, and I wanted it all! Travel, career, wild parties – tall tales to shock my grandkids. It was a high-octane life, and I liked it that way. Work hard, play harder.

This mantra became my downfall when in 2014 I burnt out. My breakdown led to my diagnosis of depression and anxiety and I was highly medicated. At 32, I moved home with my parents. It was not something I had envisioned for my life; it felt like everything was broken. Depression is like wearing a coat made of sand, with a tap constantly dripping onto it. It gets heavier and heavier until eventually, you can't bear the weight. Even seemingly simple tasks like brushing your teeth are impossible. Anxiety on the other hand is like living on a knife-edge. Imagine living your normal life exactly as it is, only you're balancing on a tightrope over a canyon. You're constantly terrified of falling off. One tiny mistake could prove fatal. Depression and anxiety hang out on a seesaw and you sway uncontrollably from one to the other. One minute you can't get off the bed, the next you're in a pool of sweat panicking about whether you remembered to take your meds. It's exhausting and I frequently contemplated ending my life.

I returned to the office nearly a year later, excited about getting my life back to normal. But in hindsight, I wasn't ready. As soon as I sat at my desk, my anxiety came rushing back. I knew at that moment something had to change. I quit on the spot. I was heartbroken and devastated for the time lost building my career.

The road to recovery was long and paved with golden trips to doctors, therapists and sobriety. Imagine a montage of Rocky running up the steps. Only the steps are covered in treacle, people are throwing rocks at him and he has no legs. By the summer of 2017, I was feeling incredible. I realised I wanted to teach the world all I had learned about healing myself and show others they could do it too.

As I began to post on social media and get the message out there, I saw motivational quotes like, "Don't be afraid to fail", "Fail forward", and "The real failure is when you stop trying". You have probably seen this type of language peppered over the popular hashtags #bossbabe, #mumpreneur, #girlboss (bleurgh!!). We use it to motivate ourselves, don't we?

"Don't be afraid to fail, Rach. Let's do this!" What codswallop! Of course, we're going to be afraid to fail. We've never run a business before and fear is bred into us.

We spend over 12 years in school, trying to please everyone by doing things right. We're taught that there is only one correct way of doing things. If you don't get it, you are a failure and you're stupid. There's no space for innovation, questioning or neurodiversity. School is a cookie-cutter, learn-off-the-page, recreated precise process. There is no room for error which means most of us grow up with the fear of getting things wrong.

This fear lingers in our subconscious along with other beliefs cemented at around the same time. Our subconscious minds are programmed in the formative years before eight; social standing is almost fully formed by the time you are twelve (which is why many people suffer from impostor syndrome); and your subconscious runs 95% of your life. Eeeeekkk!

If, like me, you found school difficult and experienced bullying, it's likely you're now a people-pleasing perfectionist with a well-tuned fear of failure. And all this is supposed to miraculously disappear overnight when your business launches? Do me a favour!

Lucky for you, I once heard a speaker at a business seminar say, "When you get comfortable, your business will suffer. Comfort is where business goes to die." So remember – if you're uncomfortable you're doing something right.

If you find yourself spiralling into negative thoughts about yourself and your business, you're not alone. Maybe that one poor customer review sticks in your mind? It's because complaints and insults hold a more significant impact than praise (you can thank your brain's in-built negativity bias for that). It's why the newspapers are full of bad news; psychologically it gets your attention over good news.

Humans are programmed to seek out safety, in order to survive. What feels safer – something new or something you've done before with a predictable outcome? The problem with safety is it traps us in behaviour that doesn't serve us.

Once I was making enough to pay all my outgoings, the original hunger I'd had for business was replaced by what I can only describe as apathy. I was tired. More clients meant more work. Why would I go looking for that? I could barely deal with everything I had on my plate already and was not going to burn out again. I stopped hankering for growth. And there is nothing wrong with that. Maybe you start with a dream of having a six, seven, even eight-figure business, but as you begin to move forward, you decide a solid five figures and more time to yourself is more your vibe.

I realised through this journey that my business is my business. No one can tell me how to run it. But conversely, no one will run it for me either. If I lose the drive for my business, the business loses its momentum. Sometimes it's OK to take a step back, slow down and enjoy what you have achieved. I find that when I rest a little, my brain thanks me for it and the hunger always comes back. So don't be afraid to get comfortable and enjoy what you've built, but don't stay too long – remember comfort is where business goes to die.

We must adapt – like Netflix which, rather than emulating the world-leader in video rentals at the time, Blockbuster, switched up its service to post out DVDs, five at a time, giving more choice and scrapping much-hated late fees. Netflix continued to innovate using emerging technology to disrupt the market with a video-streaming membership model giving us access to all content from anywhere – and leaving poor old Blockbuster filing for bankruptcy. If we don't want to end up like Blockbuster, change is scary but necessary. And change usually starts with a fearful thought of some kind.

By the end of 2018, I'd been thinking about quitting reiki for a while, so I freaked out when I decided I no longer wanted to offer it as a service – it was all I was known for. I had this gut feeling that a membership would work well so I decided to stop the reiki to make time to create it. I was terrified. What would my customers think? Would I have to start from scratch? What if it didn't work?

Newsflash: the evolution was great for my business. So don't be afraid to change things up. Be brave. Release that fear of failure and give it a go. The only way to understand what your customers want is to test the market and see the reaction.

If your product or service doesn't get the response you're looking for, try changing one of the four Ps:

People: Switch up your audience.

Product: Tweak/refresh/redo the product.

Price: Review the price point.

Place: Look at where you are selling, for example, the ad platform you're using.

Each time you "fail", you learn. You have to be OK with that. It can be soul-destroying and hard not to think, "I'm a failure" – but you are not like other business owners, you dust yourself off, get up and chuck the next idea out there. Dive out of that comfort zone and follow your gut feeling. It is usually right.

But how, Rach?!

The good thing about your most significant business asset (that astonishing muscle we call the brain) is that you can reprogramme it. I know this to be true because I have done it. Affirmations are a game-changer. They helped me build new neural pathways in my mind and you can use them too, but you need to practise daily to outweigh that negativity bias we chatted about earlier.

My top tip is to focus on what's there, not what's missing. Instead of focusing on what I don't have, which usually shows up as:

- fears around money
- being single
- approaching 40
- body shape
- my delightfully diverse brain
- not keeping on top of life admin

I focus on what I do have:

- practices which mean I don't have to take mental health medication
- a fantastic growing community
- awesome friends and a supportive family
- my health
- a business I LOVE
- food in my fridge
- clean water in my taps
- wifi

I could go on, but I'm sure you get the point.

It takes practice but as soon as I notice myself spiralling into anxiety, I simply repeat, "This is an old thought pattern. I no longer need it." I then affirm the opposite and ask my mind to bring me a more positive thought instead. This helps interrupt the thoughts and allows me to focus on the positive – but you must practise.

Think of training your mind like learning a martial art. Imagine the karate black belt shrugging their shoulders and saying, "Well, that's it, I've got to black belt level, I'll never practise again." Even at the highest level, they still practise. Why? Because without practice, there is no progress, and we feel stagnant.

Bruce Lipton says the only way to reprogramme your

subconscious mind is through hypnosis and repetition: we must repeat over and over to create new neural pathways.

When it comes to business and mindset, we expect results overnight. We have such incredibly high expectations of ourselves, like hitting six figures immediately, or reaching enlightenment the first time we try meditation. We forget about the process of progress. There is a process behind healing and getting good at business (and I believe they go hand in hand), in the same way there is a process behind getting a black belt in karate. As you learn and grow, there may be times you get punched in the face (but you learn to block those punches better each time). Maybe you'd give up? Some people do.

The winners – the people who get their black belt, or an equivalent achievement in their chosen field – have one thing in common. They practise even when it seems like progress is slow or non-existent. They trust the process. They trust that if they keep going in the right direction, they'll get where they're going. So don't freak out if you're not where you want to be just yet.

Learn to enjoy the practice and the journey instead of constantly reaching for a destination. Without training, there is no progress. It's like riding a bike, you're going to fall off and graze your knee, but if you never get back on, you won't know the joy that comes from flying down the hill with the wind in your hair screaming, "Look, Mum, no hands!!".

BIO:

Rachael focuses on empowering women to heal so they can live from a place of inner power and happiness. *Time Out* voted her one of London's best alternative therapists and her life-changing strategies, sound healings and wisdom are in demand from companies like Vans, Spotify and Weetabix, mainstream press, and podcasts like Frankie Bridge's *Open Mind*. She's driven by the transformation in her clients, often receiving handwritten cards and messages on how the tools and techniques she shares have changed lives. Rachael offers Happy Habits Club, courses, retreats and the *Things I Wish I'd Known* podcast.

www.rachaelwelford.com

CURIOSITY KILLED THE CAT

Maria Davis

I really don't like that saying. In fact, I feel it is so weighted! So charged with unseen energies that it is disturbing. Because, who wants to kill a cat after all?!!!

But having curiosity will open up your world.

One of my favourite sayings is "I wonder . . ."

You know how many things I have manifested as a result of that curiosity and those two simple words: "I wonder . . ."?

Origins of the phrase

But let's go to the origins of that phrase which will bring light to why curiosity was perceived to be a bad thing.

According to phrases.org.uk, its origin came from Ben Jonson's 1598 play, Every Man in His Humour. The phrase went like this: - *"Helter Skelter, hand sorrow, care'll kill a cat, up-tails all, and a louse for hangman".*

Then Shakespeare appropriated this link the following year from "Much Ado About Nothing" with the line: - *"What, courage man! What though care killed a cat, thou hast mettle enough in thee to kill care."*

Etymology of the word Curious

The etymology of curious begins with care c.1300 *"care, heed, from Latin care, concern trouble"* also *"means of healing, successful remedial treatment of disease"* in late 14c.

I find it fascinating in a world of "should-narratives" that we are indeed killing off the basic tools of inquiry and being wondering with the curiosity of what the world, our world, can be like. What does it have to offer when we look outside our knowing, and dive into the world of knowledge?

One of my favourite sayings is *"you know what you know, until you know something different."*

One of my most famous paths of inviting something different and extraordinary to my world is to be gently curious and wonder what my next phase or stage of evolution will be. Are you the same?

But we have this deep paradox with this simple innocuous saying that is reverberated across the unconscious collective, that being curious or wanting something more is a bad thing. It's inherent in the energy of this saying, which unfortunately sticks across many generations.

Other ways to say this:

- Know your place!
- Don't try and be someone you're not!
- Why try?

There are many paradigms across the transformation world that excavate the deep wounds of "not being enough" to fulfill your soul's mission. I am talking about the "Mother Wound, "The Good Girl Narrative", "The Witch Wound", "The Imposter Syndrome". The "Dharma Triangle", "The Acceptance and Allowance Theory", "Cognitive Behaviour Theory", "Trauma Based Somatic Therapy" and "Polyvagal Theory". You can probably think of others too. But for now, I want to shout out loud BE CURIOUS and do your inner work.

Let's debunk "not being enough" and why curiosity will lead to being the best version of you. Encourage yourself to collect evidence that anything and everything is possible. Take into consideration: *where will I put my energy today?*

Simple, innocuous phrases like this bury hope and faith across generations. Let's band together and be curious. And in the meantime, no cats will be killed on my watch. What about you?

In my work as a Spiritual Business Mentor, and indeed my time as a Medical Intuitive, I saw a lot of energy disturbance going through the physical body because people were not curious enough to dismantle some of the archaic and disturbing philosophies we buy into because of ancestry or lineage and cellular memories.

This is my work to release us all from those "should" narratives and free our spirit to be curious and wonder. Then activate your desires and destiny in the process. I know, it's a big ask!

I did it first

I was curious about what running was all about. So, at 38 years of age, I began to run long distances with a social group. I also bought into the idea of perfection and not being enough. Argh! Which brought its own curiosities. You see, curiosity is the first point, and fear, hope, and faith are the cornerstone of following through on those curiosities. I was breaking the mould on this one. No family members had ever run a marathon or even been a runner. My body was not made for long-distance running. Oh yes, there is a type. Many runners told me that I would not succeed because I did not have the body type to do long-distance running. I was curious. I kept going. This was something I needed to do.

After 5 years of running, I thought: - *"You know what? What would it be like to do a Marathon?"* Not just any Marathon, but the biggest in the world. That I would need to travel across multiple time zones, have jetlag, struggle with landing, and then do a superhuman feat. Could I do it? Of course! I was curious - remember curiosity is mixed with faith, fear, and action.

I entered the New York Marathon and low and behold finished it. That year 37000 people entered it and not all finished it, and I know that not all got to the start line either. There is a myriad of reasons why people do not go to the start or finish line. And it has a lot to do with determination, commitment, and curiosity. I wondered, what does staying in your lane look like and feel like? What if I felt like a runner? What if I connected to my soul and spirit for the necessary steps to achieve this task? How would that feel? Do I need a coach? Yes, I did, and my coach had run 89 marathons, so he had well and truly tested, his theories and practices. I asked lots of questions too. My coach and I ran the New York Marathon together. He was running his 90th and me running my 1st. The Marathon truly is a collective of the human spirit. There was a plethora of curiosity, fears, faith, and hope on the day. It is palpable. You can feel the intensity of it - it is like a wall of energy that embraces you with a warm mama hug until you reach that finish line, coaxing you the whole way. At the finish line, your arms go up and you are the only winner you need to know, like forever. Or at least for that one special life-changing and memorable moment. As a result of this superhuman feat (yep, a proven scientific fact: human form is designed to run 32km, not 42km) lots of triumphant and accomplished humans crossed the finish line. Each with their own story.

Break the mould - be curious!

I wonder if I can make money out of being a Healer. My family members were not entrepreneurs. My grandmother would heal people from the village - she would not charge so how could I? My father denied his gifts and died young because of his sensitivities.

No one wakes up with the vocation of "I want to be a healer, Mummy". You are born to be a healer. Not everyone chooses to make money and have the support of this vocation either. But I did or do!

My curiosity and sense of adventure took me to many places to refine my business model. To align with values and offer what the market needed. Healing is indeed a vocation. Business is a model and requires systems - wondering which ones fit into the healing world is to open a pandora's box. Luckily, I was fortunate enough to study with some of the wonderful teachers in the spiritual world and learned a lot. Today I run a successful healing business and teach others to do the same.

Vocations are sometimes assigned - be curious - soul mission is one of the great adventures to be curious about. Have no fear, instead be curious about what it would feel like when you step out of the confounds of the narratives you were born into. Break the mould as I did.

Energy Mastery - filter the unseen but deep self-energies

Could cosmic intelligence affect energies, physically, emotionally, mentally, and spiritually? Could it really be true that the full moon brings out all the "crazies"? Let's collect evidence. Let's be curious. Let's study the moon cycles and astrology and share common interests. Let's work on ourselves. To know what we know for certain.

I found anecdotal evidence - I've worked with 1000s of clients including my own internal work. This I know to be true: that some things are out of our reality and reach until you try and test it to be true. Including the moon and sign sun placement, and how it affects your energy. I call this the missing link. When you know the cycles and placements that affect you energetically, you can plan ahead and make sense of the world again. Be curious - it will support you in the long run.

There is a lot to learn about astrology and cosmic intelligence. Many spend lifetimes learning. There are millions across the world who have a keen interest in this body of metaphysical work. I have studied it for the last 40 years, the last 10 years in-depth and am still learning new things along the way. It is an adventure to explore the metaphysical world of the stars and the universe. Moon cycles are fascinating.

This is my LIFE Philosophy:

- Keep asking questions.
- Keep your sense of adventure alive.
- Take a new step daily.
- Be curious.
- Take a deep breath and know that your place in the world is to set a new foundation for your legacy and the legacies that come after you.
- Be who you want to see in the world.

That takes curiosity. No cats to be killed. Instead, a buoyant sense of spirit and sense of freedom to wish, dream, speak to your soul, step off the proverbial cliff and transform into the paradigm, the new YOU that takes flight and shares their journey of wisdom. So others take flight too. Curiosity will transform and ultimately heal the world.

BIO:

Maria Davis, Spiritual Business Mentor to curious Healers and Coaches who have a soul mission of healing their world to heal the world.

Source https://www.phrases.org.uk/meanings/curiosity-killed-the-cat.html
Source - https://www.etymonline.com/word/curious

www.mariaheals.com

17

THINGS I NEVER KNEW I NEEDED TO RUN MY OWN BUSINESS

Caroline Sumners

Y ou're doing what he said?
          I am giving you my letter of resignation, I repeated. Then there was a stunned silence. My manager just sat there, looking at me, not quite believing what he was hearing. I was not quite believing that I had actually done it!

It had been coming for a while.

Yes, I had just resigned from the very well-paid marketing job that I've been doing for about four years. On the surface, the job looked amazing and in many ways, it was; however, around the summer of 2013, I worked out that I'd been away travelling with work for more weekends than I had actually been at home. And I hated it!

That year, I had been to San Francisco, Moscow, Dubai, Munich, and Paris to name just a few destinations, and at one point I wasn't home for 4 weeks. Looking back now, I realise I was burnt out, but at the time I didn't realise that was even a thing.

The final push to resign came when I was complaining to my

dad about how much I was hating my job. Well, he said you better do something about it because you've got years ahead of you of work and so you better enjoy it. And of course, he was right. Plus I was starting to annoy myself with my complaints about work.

I have always been a bit of an act first, think about it later, kind of person, so about three weeks later I went in and resigned.

What's the plan?

Did I have a plan for what I was going to do? Yes. I started a travel business.

Did I have a well thought out plan for what I was going to do? Absolutely not. I started a travel business without any experience in the travel industry!!

Why would I do that?

Well, I had travelled loads and friends and colleagues were constantly asking me where they should stay in San Francisco or saying 'Hey Caroline, you've been to Barcelona. What's the best hotel to stay in?' (To this day my best travel tip in San Francisco is taking the first boat of the day to Alcatraz and when you go inside as everyone else goes right, peel off and go left and you end up in solitary confinement on your own. It is eerily impressive.)

I had also spent years organising events, conferences, and business incentives in multiple locations around the world, so I had a good idea about what people want in a holiday or business travel.

Therefore, my idea was to offer a fully supported event and conference venue finding solution, complete with the ability to book all the travel and additional organisation that companies might need. Just the sort of service I had needed in my job. I never intended to start a travel agency for individuals to book holidays. And yet about 6 to 8 months into starting the business that is where I found myself.

I was frustrated I had gone off course so easily, and pretty soon I found myself drifting back to marketing. I kept getting asked by previous colleagues if I was doing any marketing work and so alongside the travel business I took on marketing.

I read somewhere once that you should not try to change career and industry at the same time, and here I was trying to change industry and career and start a business all in one go. On top of this, the travel industry is, I believe, a broken model. As a consumer, you don't pay for the expertise of a travel agent. Instead, the travel agent is remunerated via a commission model from hotels, airlines, etc. What this results in is a complete devaluing of the skills and knowledge that an agent has. Very often I would get enquiries from somebody wanting help organising their honeymoon, do a day's worth of work finding them the perfect hotel, flights, and location only for them to turn around and say thanks very much, but I've booked it myself online for £100 cheaper. It was beyond frustrating.

As a result of my frustration, about a year after I've started the travel business I was completely rethinking what I was doing. Honestly, I felt a bit like a failure. I had gone into this new business full of enthusiasm and within months it was falling apart, and I was on the verge of giving up.

Time for a rethink

I had come to realise that I hadn't fallen out of love with marketing as I thought when I resigned from my job. Instead, it was the culture and the company that I was working for that I didn't love!

After about two years of being in business, I was doing two jobs alongside each other – trying to maintain the travel business whilst at the same time getting more marketing work.

Eventually, I closed the travel business completely. Really I should have closed it sooner than I did, but I didn't want to admit that I had made a mistake or that it hadn't worked. My ego definitely got in the way.

Starting a business that you then decide to close is a humbling experience, but ultimately, I made the decision to close the travel business because I was hanging onto it; I didn't want to admit I had made a mistake. One thing I learned though is that you need to make these decisions as quickly as you can.

Hanging onto something that is not lighting you up and isn't serving you, just brings you down. At the back of my mind, I also felt like I wasn't serving the travel customers I had, well enough.

If you google 'failure quotes' they are pretty much of a theme of, do it fast. I took the practical approach and did just that.

Lessons Learnt

Along the way I have made mistakes and learnt a few things, so here are my tips for running a successful business. (in no particular order)

1. Embrace failure. I know it's a cliche but in order to improve, you need to embrace failure. For a long time I viewed my failed travel business as something to be ashamed of. Now I can view it much more objectively, which helps me serve my clients so much better. I did not do enough research around the business I was building or whether it was a service that potential clients really wanted – it was based mostly on gut and guesswork.
2. Find your tribe. Many people who know me have heard the story about how I used to go round to the Co-op around the corner from my flat just to talk to

people. Only when I found a co-working space over a year into my business did I feel like I had support from other people who understood what it is like to run your own business. Now I have 'campfires' with four amazing humans, and we talk and leave voice notes for each other about just about anything. It was a year before we even met in person.

3. Don't try to do too many things at once. I've learnt the hard way that in order to be successful you need to focus on one business at a time. Your mind simply becomes overloaded. Well, mine does, anyway.

4. Know your numbers. I cannot emphasise this enough!

5. Trust your gut.

6. Only work with people you like. Trust me on this one!

7. Ethics is more important than ever.

8. Mindset is everything. If you don't have this right you will get stuck in inactivity.

9. Hustle mentality is dead (to me); go quietly at your own pace.

10. Imposter syndrome, which I never knew about until I ran my own business, can stop you from taking action. Take steps to recognise it and overcome it.

11. Resilience is underrated but critical.

12. If you don't love your business then no one else is going to either.

13. Make decisions quickly – but make sure you have done the work on research first. When I am working with clients now on their marketing plans, this is always the bit that they had skipped before working with me.

14. Have confidence in your ability. It is so easy to second guess yourself. Don't!

15. Sack clients who don't pay you on time. Honestly. It

seems harsh, but if they don't respect you enough to pay you on time, then do not work with them.

16. Running your own business isn't the easiest path, but it's definitely the most interesting one.

17. Consistency, consistency, consistency. Even if consistency is 1 x per week or 1 x per month, just do it and commit to it.

18. Pay yourself first.

19. Don't rely on social media platforms as the only connection with your customers. Own the relationship. This is becoming even more important as social platforms evolve.

20. You don't have to be on every social media platform. Yes Tik~Tok is huge, but if your clients are not there, don't waste your time

21. Plan time off in your diary months in advance. For years I didn't do this, and I found that I ended up crashing and burning out.

22. Set boundaries and embrace saying no! This is a tough one. But very, very important.

23. Ask questions.

24. Listen to answers.

25. Get dressed. It's a downward spiral when you sit in your pyjamas all day! Trust me. I know.

26. Shop local and support other small businesses (always).

27. Remove ego.

28. Take a break and get a coffee.

BIO:

Caroline Sumners is a Marketing Mentor and Online Business Consultant working with service-based and e-commerce business owners who are stuck and stagnant with not enough sales. She is a certified conscious consultant with proven systems and frameworks and 20+ years' experience in marketing. Caroline lives on the Hampshire coast with her Miniature Schnauzer Rufus.

www.carolinesumners.com

18

IT IS ALL ABOUT THE STORY

Monique Gaudion

A s the self-assured purple cow that I am, I will be sharing with you today, just how easy it can be to apply practical emphasis in the art of storytelling to bring in vast and fast success in business branding and networking.

Back before my business career took flight, when theatre and touring balanced precariously with my day job, where life and my ideas were nothing but possibilities, I had a dream. A literal dream about a woman who wore masks throughout her life to find acceptance, to get by. A woman who finds a new balance, igniting a surge of inspiration and an awareness of who she is. I was at a crossroads where two distinct aspects of life: the necessity of paying the bills and a burning desire and career align. The dream unleashed possibility, creativity, and passion for life in the form of a business in the creative industries. I remembered that woman in my dream, I took a leap, wrote a one woman show and suddenly, playfully, my potential ignited. Thus was the birth of my creative entertainment design company, Way Out Theatreworks.

I was a business virgin when I first started. I knew nothing. It started with multitudes of cold calls and a couple of editorial pieces in the local paper which gained me private and small business clients. My goal was to get into the Conference and Events Industry. Boy was I green. I joined an industry networking group and being a newbie, I was ignored. I was yet to prove myself. I'd sidle up to a group chatting and as I had nothing to contribute, I would just listen. I was pretty much invisible for the first couple of years, but I took in all they shared. The highs and lows, what was new and how the industry worked.

I did not go away and eventually they asked me what I did. My god was I excited! Finally, I got to give my well-practiced elevator speech. They were not interested. In time I stopped selling, relaxed and I put into practice what I was doing in my business and that was providing experiences. I had learnt the art of storytelling to not only gain credibility but the ability to win clients. I no longer listed the services my company provided. I simply told them stories from my past events, stories relevant to them.

What do I mean by that? We are so keen to get the business that we often dive right in and start telling our potential client what we do, how good our services, packages, and products are. We forget the art of silence and how we can best help them by taking the time to listen. I know this is not new advice, but in my eagerness to help these potential clients, I erroneously found myself doing all the talking and convincing. Not a great start.

But no, after all that fussing, it was the simple art of listening that gained me access to high profile clients such as Coca Cola, BP, top five banks, major universities, Government agencies like ASIC and conference organisers. It was active listening. I didn't just wait till they stopped talking and jump in. I asked questions. Once I understood their needs, their misgivings, or uncertainties, I could respond with the story that could alleviate those concerns and meet their needs.

Here are some examples. If a client were a little nervous about booking an immersive entertainment event for their Christmas party, unsure their staff would get involved and though they did not say it, concerned they would get blamed if it went pear shaped. I would tell them a story of a department from a "well known" hospital for whom I did their Christmas party. On arrival, all dressed up in their costumes, instead of nervous excitement, this group stood stiffly in a circle. I was confident in my program so, we continued on. The group of forty people had a wonderful time, with people supporting each other, sharing in laughter, all that stiffness and reserve melted away. The organiser later told me how shocked she was at how well it went because half the people were not talking to each other, and some had professional complaints pending on those staff at the event.

If they were concerned their event wouldn't be memorable, I would tell them of an occasion in Central Hong Kong when a person called out to me as I was crossing the street. I knew him from an event one year prior. He proceeded to wax lyrical about the whole experience and how their event became, to quote him, 'the talk of Hong Kong.'

What about if something went wrong, or they had a tricky/fussy boss. I would tell them of a Murder Party I ran for a well-known international vehicle company. The guests were to be fifty-five men and only fifteen women. As most murder parties are close evenly 50/50 male/female, I suggested we dress fifteen men in drag. They excitedly agreed and I provided costumes for seventy people, with fifteen men in frocks, wigs, stockings, jewellery and even bras! It was hilarious! There was one problem though, the General Manager had not appeared, and we needed to start. I spoke to his assistant and long story short; he didn't like his dress. Thankfully, I had a snazzy red number ready to go, so I offered it up and he was happy. Of course, it was not the dress giving him doubt, it was him in his hotel room staring at the mirror dressed in drag! But sure enough, he presented himself as the leader he was and bravely came down to the party. Once he saw all the other guys in drag and greeted by his staff with cheers, he relaxed, and the party went on to be a huge hit. I loved that event.

What about the biggest event I pitched for in my career? An international summit hosted by the Lord Mayor of Brisbane. Not only was I to write and produce the opening performance but I was to supply entertainment day and night for all four days of the Summit. The opening production had forty performers, including multicultural acts, multimedia – it was huge. It went for tender and I, a small company, was up against some of the biggest and best in Queensland. And how did I win the booking? You guessed it, sharing stories from past events. After the opening production, the Lord Mayor left his table of dignitaries, came backstage and shook my hand telling me how impressed he was with the show. Not only that he wrote me a letter acknowledging the impact my contribution had to the success of the Summit. Now, that is a story to tell a client who is unsure of my credentials.

The lesson here is I could have just told potential clients the program or services I could provide, but to what impact? Far better a relevant and truthful experience that will alleviate any fear or hesitation they may have in hiring a company they have never used before. Even more pertinent if your services are costly, which mine were.

This also applies to networking. Listening is the active process of receiving and responding to spoken (and sometimes unspoken) messages. Not only that, but it is also remembering. So, pay attention to chit chat. It is all significant. Clients and connections come from relationships; that is the language of business.

Telling a story by how you present yourself. I am sure you have heard of Seth Godin's book 'Purple Cow'? If not, I highly recommend it. If you drove past one hundred jersey cows, you would not notice any one cow. If you saw a purple cow, now that cow would get your attention. It is remarkable. I worked in the industry of corporate and Govt. bodies. They all dressed in dark suits. They looked fabulous. I represented the creative industries to their world. I needed to dress with elements both creative and professional. Stand out but not for the wrong reasons. I found my personal purple cow. People remembered me. I had energy, I listened, I had stories, I was unique and presented as a specialist. It worked. Find your purple cow-ness. You are a story. You are repeatedly conveying to people who you are and what you represent. What you think about your past and your present I guarantee you, will be your future.

My last story is really the first chapter of my new story; I am the host of the Boffola Podcast. For those hesitant to come onto the podcast I share a story and here is one. I had two architects to come on the show. I had prepped them to have a story or two at hand. On the day, prior to hitting record I asked them if they had their stories and they said "No, we thought it was an interview." I had no questions prepared but thankfully I thrive on improvisation and had confidence it would fall into place. They went on to share amazing experiences in creating an exclusive luxury eco-safari lodge in Botswana. We all agreed it went very well. One of the two later told me "I forgot we were even doing a podcast." Now, that was music to my ears because that is how I love my guests to feel. Relaxed and enjoying the experience.

Business can be fun, and it certainly is creative. Providing experiences and connections continues to be fun and exhilarating. Way Out Theatreworks' clients had positive experiences and came back repeatedly. They referred me to others, and that is how I got new clients. As for the Boffola Podcast, well I have no doubt that it will have a similar tale as we travel together, both guests and listeners; lifted high on the wings of the curious and the joyful stories.

Humans have been telling stories as long as we have had language. We think in stories, remember in stories, and turn just about everything we experience into a story. Stories and connections - it is where we find joy in business and life.

BIO:

Monique Gaudion founded Way Out Theatreworks, a multi award-winning innovative company well recognised for integrating creativity and excellence providing unique bespoke entertainment experiences and productions to the private, corporate and government sectors. Her love of story is an international one, spanning over 25 years writing, performing, producing shows and events that embody emotions and experiences that inspire creativity and connection. In 2021 Monique turned her love of story and communication into the Boffola Podcast. A down to earth welcoming space for shared stories that honours connection, vulnerability, inspiration, courage, and of course, being Monique, much laughter.

www.linkedin.com/in/moniquegaudion

19

YOU ARE EVERYTHING YOU
NEED TO START A BUSINESS

Siobhan Fox

P eople start a business for a multitude of reasons - maybe it's because life leaves them few other choices, or perhaps because they have a vision that can't be ignored. For some, maybe it's a bit of both. If I'm honest with myself, that's probably me! If you're reading this book, I'd take a guess that something within you yearns to follow this path too. You want to help people solve a specific kind of problem in a totally unique way, you want to make people smile, you want to bring a little ray of sunshine into someone's day. If that sounds like you, then I'll also take a guess that you've identified that your audience are in some kind of pain and you have a great way to alleviate it. Why? Well, because you know some really important things about that pain, don't you?

Whether you know it or not, whether you have qualifications or accreditations to prove it, your life experience to date has led you to a deep understanding of this problem your business idea is going to solve. You've been working on it whilst you've spent time in every totally unrelated job, whilst you've been succeeding and failing, ending relationships and forming new ones, dreaming of the future and healing from the past. Whilst you've been living.

It turns out that everything you know about that problem you could help people solve, and everything you bring into building a business, is not just about what you'd put on a CV. In fact, the greatest skills you bring to the table right now are down to your entire life experience. Travelling, supporting friends and family, going to art galleries, breaking off relationships, parenting, reading books, getting into debt, meeting new people, failing, flying, listening, speaking... how much have you learned about what it means to be a human being? Picture it all: written in a book, or as a collection of podcasts, or as a film. There would be reels and reels of experiences, memories, reflections and lessons learned. What you need to know, what you really really need to know, is that people will pay you money to tap into all of that amazing stuff, not just the qualifications, skills or training courses you've been on. When you hear 'people buy people!' in a business context, this is what they are really talking about: all the other amazing things that you have inside that exceptional brain of yours.

Real talk: doing this business-owning thing by yourself, or with a small team, is hard. There's no sugar-coating it. We are not only the delivery department, the hands-on people creating and delivering the thing we sell, but we are also the Finance Dept, Sales Dept, HR Dept, Admin Dept, Marketing Dept, R&D Dept, Customer Services/Client Management, plus of course The Board! We're the CEO, Chairman, Heads of Department and every single person underneath. So if you find yourself feeling overloaded, like your to do lists keep mutating into multiple lists with a plethora of arms and legs, just know you're not alone!

So with all of these departments to both run, and be, where do we turn? How do we remove the mental clutter and bring more balance, space and time into our lives, so we can enjoy the day to day and implement more of our brilliant ideas?

I guess this is the moment where I tell you my story, because I've been there. Hell, I'm still there sometimes! The thing is; success looks different for each of us. It's also not a destination, it's a *process*. No business owner magically wakes up one day and proudly proclaims to their family "I've made it!" The business owner's journey is just a succession of peaks and troughs, where we hope that the overall average, results in an upward trajectory. How you measure that trajectory is individual to you based on your own values, life experience and priorities. For me it's about maintaining stable mental health. That is my absolute priority and biggest driver of every business decision I make, because I've actually stood on the peak of a mountain that looked very much like "I've made it", earning nearly six figures in a high profile corporate job, and then slid straight into one of my life's deepest troughs. I burned out. I burned out really hard and really fast, but when I reflect I see that it had been building for a while. The signs of struggle were there, but I didn't believe I had options. Sticking a brave face on and swallowing my pain would only last for so long.

I've been through a lot in my career - I've experienced a lot of bullying, sexual discrimination and gaslighting. I've eaten a lot of shit, from both men and women, and it took me until I hit my 30s to start to believe that there might be another way to get ahead. Then I had a baby and my world turned 180 degrees. Nearly 19 years of 40 - 50 hour weeks and giving my career my all became irrelevant overnight. I was thrown into a 24-hour-a-day almost-impossible job with zero training, where there were no lunch breaks, no appraisals, no direction, no ideas. And worse than that, this was the most important job I had ever done. I couldn't just bust out an 'oops sorry, my bad' when I fucked up. A split-second mistake could literally be the difference between life and death. (Ask me about the time my son managed to roll off a bed at 4 months and we triggered safe-guarding procedures when we took him to hospital to have him checked over!).

Sadly, for me, my early experiences of motherhood were overwhelmingly sad, painful and anxiety-inducing. It started with a long labour culminating in an emergency C-section, then a mostly unpleasant and painful experience of breastfeeding, an intensely unhappy baby with a scream that could shatter glass, and all without any real day-to-day support. My other friends snuggled up with their babies, enjoying afternoon coffee and cake with friends, cooing at them whilst they happily fed from the boob or a bottle. I sat sweating, gripping my seat in fear that my son would want feeding, or would need a nap, or would just decide to have an endless unexplained screaming fit. Every time I bailed out of a situation, tears of frustration streaming down my cheeks, I would ask myself what was wrong with me. Why didn't other people's babies scream like their very souls were on fire? What was I doing wrong? It felt like everyone else with babies was one side of a pane of glass, whilst my son and I were on our own, inside a dark, lonely prison of our own making.

I look back now and of course, I can see we were stuck in an endless loop of anxiety together. He triggered me, I triggered him and so it went on. Of course things eventually improved - he and I could go out and do things together without me always having to plan an exit strategy. Then just as I started to feel some of the real joy of being a mother, of watching a chunky cheeky baby learning to clap and crawl and chuckle with glee, my return to work rushed up to slap me in the face. I "couldn't afford" to go part time, and so reluctantly I tried to return to my 40 hour weeks, my 4 hours a day of commuting. I tried to return to my previous 'work life' and of course, with a one year old in nursery full time, the wheels fell off. I crashed out with anxiety so bad I struggled to leave the house, and for a while everything was in tatters. I couldn't do my job, I couldn't be a good mum, I couldn't remember who I was. It was a dark, cold, lonely time.

But after the winter comes the spring, and eventually new seeds began to sprout. I started applying for local jobs, meeting new people, nervously attending local networking meetings. A dream began to form; a new vision of a new life. Not just a new life, but a new way of life. With everything I had ever worked for and believed, in pieces on the floor at my feet, I got to choose what I picked back up. With every new experience, new friend or connection, my self-esteem slowly came back online and this new vision came into sharper focus. I would work 3 days a week, spend 2 with my little boy and the weekends would be family time. It would be the perfect balance of my time - giving us all about the right amounts of what we needed.

I started off how many consultant-types do and I sold all my available hours to one client. It was a fantastic experience to step inside a small business and provide them with hands-on marketing support, but a couple of months in, I found myself burning out yet again. I asked myself: how did I end up here? And with the help of a business coach, I discovered where I could improve. The single biggest thing it came down to was that I could not continue to directly trade my time for money. I had to learn how to see my value as more than just my time.

This is the single biggest learning I want to share with you, regardless of where you are in your entrepreneurial journey: you do not have to directly trade your time for money. You can absolutely price services or products according to their value to the client or customer. It is no one's business but yours how long those services or products take to create or deliver. You have spent years honing your skills, your technique, gathering your incredible life experience. If you can deliver something in an hour, it's because you have spent time learning how to do it in an hour. If you're going to deliver a 2 hour workshop, you've got a few hours' work either side of that you need to charge for.

Let go of the notion that people won't pay you for what you create or what you know. No one in the world knows what you know, has seen what you've seen, or experienced what you've experienced. You are a UNIQUE individual, remember!? The real truth of business is that people will pay you money for the absolutely incredible uniqueness of YOU, trust me. It's time for you to go forth and be awesome, my friend, because I 100% believe in you!

BIO:

Siobhan Fox is a self-confessed marketing nerd, aspiring author, wild swimmer, mother, cheese-lover and owner of two businesses. The first - Reveal Marketing - supports small businesses to create the marketing strategy they need to achieve their goals. Siobhan also mentors other small business owners to make more money in less time, and hosts the Unconventional Business Academy - a business membership community for real people to build real businesses in the real world.

www.revealmarketinguk.com

20
FROM SAILOR TO SELLER

Johanna Hooper

Picture the scene. It's 2018. I've been a management consultant for 4 years, generating over a million pounds in sales every year, highly in demand by clients, and earning a 6 figure salary. Prada handbags all round, darling! **SUCCESS**!! Or, was it? I was also commuting 20 hours a week between Southampton and London, was knackered at weekends and didn't see much of the famalam. Half of that salary was spent on the 'pleasure' of commuting to London or paying for services that I didn't have time to do myself, like cleaning. Something had to change.

So far, so normal for many small business starting out stories. With a slight difference. This would be the second major career change I'd subjected myself to in less than 5 years!! You see, before 2018, I'd spent 23 years in the Royal Navy. Doing nothing even vaguely related to business development, commercial management or any other 'business-y' things. And here I was contemplating doing it again. Was I mad?? Well, maybe a bit. But I also loved the idea of being in charge of my own destiny and having more say over the who/how/what/when of my job. So with my big pants on, and my heart in my hands, I left my safe, lucrative employment and went out on my own. Gulp.

When I left consulting I had no clue what EXACTLY I was going to do. Instead, I had three, what I called, "lines of enquiry" that I wanted my business to be about; teaching, coaching and public speaking. All with the same end goal – to help people be BRILLIANT! Those were the things that I enjoyed doing so wouldn't it be cool to spend all my time doing just that!

I then set about gaining qualifications and accreditations that supported those lines of enquiry. It's always been important to me that I am a 'safe pair of hands' in my coaching. So I not only gained qualifications in coaching and mentoring, but also accreditation with the European Mentoring and Coaching Council (EMCC). It basically means that some very nice person has put me through my paces and decided that I can be trusted to help other people. Phew!

I set up Limitless Peak Performance on 4 February 2019, so I'm now officially a toddler! I know, I know, the name is a bit of a mouthful isn't it? Even more amusing, I wanted to capture this idea that our development opportunities are *limitless*, and then I set myself up as a limited company…. So the pursuit of limitless development opportunities is, in fact, limited (facepalm!). Add to 'To Do List' – consider changing name of business….

But, despite the utter mouthful and oxymoron that is my business name, I do firmly believe that we can all reach our own peak performance – I've certainly come a long way from the two naff A Levels I left school with! I knew back then, and I still agree now, that I couldn't have gone straight from the Royal Navy into running my own business. I needed a safe place to unlearn/relearn who I was without stripes and a gold-trimmed tricorn and not worry about where the next pay cheque was coming from whilst I did that. I learnt so much about business development and proposal writing while employed plus it helped hone my strengths into ones that work in 'Civvy Street'.

My journey as a business owner has been an interesting one, and even more so thanks to good old Covid-19. I'm pretty sure that hot on the heels of the hospitality industry, the learning and development sector is also a significant casualty of war as that's often the first bit of discretionary spend that gets ditched in a crisis!

For my first year in business I relied heavily on associate delivery relationships that helpfully funded all the things I wanted to do for my business like websites and branding. Unhelpfully, these opportunities died instantly at the onset of the first lockdown as organisations laid off staff or stopped using folks like me. The great thing about this associate work is that it was lucrative enough to carry me financially through 2020. The bad thing was that it had stopped me focussing on building MY business. At that time, only about 15% of my revenue was self-generated. The blessing of Covid is that it has turned that around and now 100% of my revenue is self-generated, albeit of a slightly smaller revenue figure. But, it's all mine……. And I couldn't be more proud.

My real passion is actually blending my two major beliefs:

- everyone has the potential to be AMAZING, they just need to be motivated in the right way; and
- everyone has a right to be led by good leaders, who care about them and their success.

Blending these together, I have focussed my coaching on helping small business owners grow their businesses, staying safe and sane in the process, by learning how to find and lead a team they can rely on. Through some of the work I do with

Portsmouth and Winchester Universities, it's really apparent how some businesses are trying desperately to lead a successful and growing business with little in the way of learning to help them. So that's my mission.

In the Navy we talked about leadership all the time. It was omnipresent because we knew how much of a gamechanger it could be. I'd love to build that same level of consciousness in the small business community, making it something we all add to our, "Be better at xxxxx....." lists. I want to make it ok for folks to stick their hands up and admit that they could do this leadership 'thing' even better tomorrow. I want to normalise asking for help with leadership and bring it out of the shadows. We are more than happy to admit we are not very arty/creative/innovative etc. How about admitting that we've made some leadership booboos in our times? I certainly have – ask me one day about the performance management discussion that ended with the individual running out of my cabin in tears.......

Since setting up my business I have also incorporated mediation and conflict coaching into my list of services. These to me were no brainers because leadership is basically all about the relationships we have with the people around us in our businesses. I do lots of public speaking events all about my favourite topic – which is resilience. I use the story of a sinking ship that I was serving on in the Royal Navy (have I told you this one? Well, long story short, I nearly died.......) to bring to life our stress triggers, our responses and why our stress deserves diagnosis™ before we decide how to mitigate it. Take a look at my talk on Ted.com if you are intrigued!

In the time I've been in business I have:

- Delivered over 400 hours of group and 121 coaching

and been accredited as a Senior Practitioner with the EMCC;

- Helped people from all walks of life (including pilots, NHS staff, HR Directors, Financial Advisers and even Tree Surgeons!) and at all levels achieve their peak performance;
- Spoken at numerous conferences such as a Defence Wider Leadership Forum, an Air Safety Conference, a Women in Defence UK 10-year anniversary conference and even (can you believe it!!!) been a TEDx speaker;
- Held numerous teaching events where I help people develop personalised resilience building plans (did I mention I was once on a sinking ship?!);
- Worked, pro bono, with Cancer Research UK and Resilient Pilot – 2 charities that are doing amazing things and have amazing people to work with!

I absolutely love my job and the value I bring to my clients! I never get the Sunday night blues or wish I could stay in bed. I get such joy at witnessing the fabulous humans that reach their version of AMAZING and having a small part to play in that transformation. I have started coaching assignments where there has been lots of tears and hopelessness, and ended in places none of us could have imagined! Like the pilot working in a chicken shed who hadn't flown for 2 years now back in the air and loving life again.

So, what's next? Well, *ooooooobviously* I have some revenue growth goals I'm hoping to reach..... (are you listening Covid 19??) And I'd love to become known as the "go to gal" for small business leadership. But that may be a way off yet!

So in the meantime:

- I'll keep doing the mentoring and teaching with as many business schools that will have me.
- I'm launching my new programme in Q2 of 2022 (hey, that rhymes!). It takes business owners wanting to transition from 'solopreneur to team' on a journey that will help them learn how to communicate with, motivate and delegate to folks that may not look, smell or think like them!
- I'll continue to work with those two amazing charities, and
- I'll find as many folks as possible that I can help be their version of AMAZING!

BIO:

Johanna Hooper is a small business leadership coach helping build the competence and confidence of those business owners looking to move from just 'little old them' in their business to leading a happy and productive team that delivers excellence at all times. So they can go off and play golf. Or whatever else it is that they would rather be doing.

www.limitlesspeakperformance.co.uk

21
IF YOU CHANGE NOTHING,
NOTHING CHANGES

Anouska Grist

I nearly died once.

(Maybe I should rephrase this…) I had tried to end my life many times over the years, but this time, I almost succeeded. After a huge overdose, taking absolutely everything in our medicine cupboard, I was rushed to Winchester hospital, where I consequently had a fit and started choking on my own tongue which obstructed my airways for too long…

As cliché as it sounds, I did indeed start 'fading' along darkness, feeling a sense of relief and comfort as I felt compelled to move closer to a 'glow' of light to the right of me. As I inched toward it, I stopped, then heard a voice that sounded like me but wasn't me. It said "you don't want to die. You aren't ready." followed by "…you just don't want to be in the situation you're in…".

I started hearing frantic voices to the left of me, that got louder, until I was back in the room with the nurses and doctors, laying on a bed (there's hope and happiness at the end of this chapter, I promise you!).

It took all of this for me to start making changes to my life, and to start living.

I had experienced my father suddenly dying when I was 13, which I couldn't accept or grieve properly from, leaving my mother to pick up the pieces (she's fabulous, and mum, if you're reading this, I'm so grateful for you always being there) with our family life, and then, a traumatic event at the age of 17 that started an avalanche leading to my mental health hitting rock bottom.

I never talked to anyone about it, nor did I report the incident (as I truly believed that it was my own fault for putting myself into the situation in the first place), which procured years of confusing emotions. Guilt. Self hatred. Pain. I didn't want to 'feel' any more.

I started eating and drinking more than what is considered normal so as to deal with my emotions, which led to me ballooning from a size 12 to a 16 very quickly.

18 and at college studying music tech (I so wanted to be a vocalist. I can reach some pretty high notes!), I fell pregnant. Finally settling on my decision to have my baby, I started eating for 5 people... which led to me weighing in at 18st 1lb and a size 22-24 after I had her...

Life after birth wasn't how I imagined it would be... My partner was aggressive and abusive on many levels which I have since forgiven and put behind me, because holding a grudge is like drinking poison and expecting the other person to die. Animosity eats away at us.

I became very fixated on my weight and lost a tremendous amount in less than a year. The equivalent of a person... I shrunk down to 9 and a half stone, then decided to let my sadness at my situation further fuel this. I was literally surviving on one biscuit, cups of tea, one options hot chocolate and 4 mouthfuls of my evening meal in a day, then started purging everything I ate, THEN restricted further and was only eating half of a low fat yoghurt in a day. My body went down to 6st 7lbs and I was a UK size 4-6. I was in a lot of emotional pain and was prescribed different types of antidepressants and antipsychotics at varying strengths, which kept seeing me try to end myself.

I wasn't the best mother I could be to my daughter Phoebe. I was too young, still too selfish, dealing with multiple traumas, and even though I always kept her fed and clean, took her to mother and baby groups and she was still raised by me to an extent, she would often go and stay with my mum so that I could secretly honour the eating disorder in me, to go out, get drunk and be reckless, further feeding the metaphorical giant toxic band aid I was holding over my emotional wounds. I managed to recover from anorexia and bulimia, but the voices of these disorders still rear their ugly heads on occasions.

Then... I fell into drug use... and formed some habits.

This brings us back to where I started writing about how I nearly died and how I'd decided that I was going to leave my children's father.

At first it was small steps, but I fully made the leap in 2012 and had a very wild time of the next several months as a newly single lady, alongside a friend who is now my closest and best friend, and whom had also recently separated from her long term partner, and our friendship soon blossomed into a group, as we attracted more friends, forming what we referred to as 'Satan's Bitches'. We would turn up at gigs and dance in our carefree way, encouraging people onto the dance floor to join us, which led to us getting consistent requests to attend gigs.

We had a very distinctive look, with our crazy backcombed hair complete with brightly coloured streaks, tattoos, piercings and punk rock attire. Music and gigs became our life, but along with this came alcohol, smoking and for me, drugs...

I met and fell for an utter charmer who at that time was the most gorgeous man I had ever laid eyes on with his tattoos, toned frame, slicked back hair and modern rockabilly style. He was a keen skateboarder and loved rock and punk music. I fully fell for him and tortured myself because I wasn't confident enough to determine with him what we actually were in terms of a relationship. I felt wild when I was with him, smoking more, drinking beer in bed first thing when we woke up. Then, he broke my heart. I pined for him, and tortured myself with the grief I was feeling at this 'whateveritwas' ending.

I was drinking more and more, smoking as and when I could, shoving substances up my nose at any opportunity. Because I was functioning daily, I was unaware of how I was gradually sinking further into addiction, putting myself in situations where I left myself vulnerable. In my head I felt I was being 'strong' and independent, numbing, silencing, blotting out all the traumas I had experienced.

Months rolled by and I couldn't shake this lonely feeling of despair as I drank and smoked my evenings away whilst my two daughters were asleep in bed. Anything to not have to deal with my thoughts.

Then, as I was sat on the bus, I was introduced to someone through my best friend. A man she had previously had a fling with (but it didn't work out) and told me he was a really decent guy. 'Richard'. I took his number and sent him a text. We arranged to meet for the first time later that evening for a drink.

I stood nervously outside the bar, awaiting his company, then we both went in together. Being the judgemental person I was back then, I immediately wasn't attracted to him, and thoughts of 'he's too old for me' 'we'll have nothing in common' and more crossed my mind.

Well... we spent the entire evening chatting non-stop, and

found that we had lots in common! (9 years on I'm still with this man and we share a daughter, 'Nova', who inspired me to create my business!)

On my birthday in January 2014 my life changed forever. I was out with friends without my partner on yet another drunken session celebrating and decided to carry on the party back at my house (my children were staying with their father for the weekend), where we played strip poker and carried on drinking. After the game finished, I drunkenly stumbled upstairs to fetch some comfortable PJ's, unaware that one of our party had followed me up the stairs and into my bedroom. He walked up behind me and sexually assaulted me. Not knowing what to do in this situation, and not wanting to cause a fuss, I made the excuse that I was tired and needed to go to bed, managing to get past him and walk down the stairs, telling the rest of the group that I needed to sleep and that I needed them to go.

Finally alone, I went and curled up in my bed, numb, trying to make sense of what had just happened, how a friend of mine could have stepped over this line.

I never wanted to be this vulnerable to anyone ever again. No more alcohol.

This was the huge turning point in my life when I knew I needed to face up to my past traumas, and I successfully did so, talking for the first time out loud about what happened when I was 17, about the recent incident, about everything. Then I forgave myself, for it was out of my control. I finally felt free.

One month after I'd quit alcohol, I fell very ill, and was misdiagnosed with Fibromyalgia as well as Crohn's disease. This sparked an interest in natural healing and I started researching ways to heal myself, stumbling across information on a wholefoods plant-based diet. I switched overnight to this way of eating and within several weeks was back to myself.

I became interested in becoming a nutritional biochemist, so returned to college, embarking on a higher learning course for adults. Achieving A level qualifications, I started at university, and fell ill again, but this time it was worse... after extensive tests and much pushing from me for answers, I had MRI tests and was diagnosed with MS and Coeliac Disease in 2016. I decided to defer from university because it was too much, and so focused on healing myself once again, this time through diet and targeted supplementation of vitamins and amino acids. I succeeded, which led me to extend my research into other areas of the body that could be healed naturally.

January 2017, my partner and I decided to have a child together which led to heartache as we lost our baby girl, 'Mia', in utero, which was the most painful experience I have ever gone through. Months later, I was carrying our little girl 'Nova', and I was certain I was going to do everything as natural as possible. I noted a distinct lack of talc alternatives, so embarked on creating my own to use on Nova after she was born, which led to me starting my business 'NovaPure Naturals'. Along my journey into business, feedback from customers has shown that I formulated a somewhat miracle product that heals a myriad of skin conditions!

My journey to where I am now in life is testimony that no matter where you start, that no matter what life throws at you, that you ARE an amazing being and that you CAN make a success of your life.

Take that leap, because there is no worse feeling than regret.

You just need to have faith in yourself.

BIO:

Anouska Grist is the owner and founder of NovaPure Naturals with her innovative flagship product being what her business is best known for, due to its capability to heal multiple skin complaints. A believer in the power of positive thinking,

Anouska is a strong fan of mindfulness and the law of attraction. Anouska is also mother to three daughters, is a classically trained vocalist and part-time model who can often be found in the kitchen playing alchemist with food to create unusual yet delicious wholefood plant based recipes.

www.novapurenaturals.co.uk

22
PAY YOURSELF FIRST

Karima Mckenzie-Thomas

I f you read Volume 3 of this powerful book series, you know I had the awesome opportunity of contributing to that book, and sharing a slice of my story. Well, Trudy - via a series of interesting twists and turns - gave me the amazing opportunity to contribute to this volume too!! WHOOOHOOOO!!!! So... here I go again.

In my Volume 3 chapter I spoke about Purpose - those small, seemingly insignificant things that we do for others moment to moment, which brighten their moods, shift their perspectives, and in fact, change their lives! Because Purpose isn't a big, loud, name in lights and face on billboards thing. Rather, it is the tiny, every day conscious actions that snowball into a well-lived life of memorable positive impact!

In this chapter, I'd like to talk about Purpose, but from a totally different perspective. I'd like you to join me in interrogating Purpose in your OWN life. What do I mean by that? Glad you asked!

Pay Yourself First.

Usually when we hear those words, we immediately think Money. 10%, 20%, etc, of our income going into a long term interest earning account that we never touch. And yes, that's very important. But, that's not at all what I'm talking about here.

What would paying yourself first look like, if money wasn't in the equation? How should you pay yourself first, **every day** and **in every interaction**? Let's talk about it.

Because of my childhood and teenage years trauma, although I was the outgoing, bubbly, life of the party, take care of everyone else girl, I was also the low self-worth, lacking healthy boundaries, low emotional quotient (EQ) girl.

As bubbly as I was, I could get to 1000 real quick! As effervescent as I was, I struggled with being in deeply toxic intimate relationships for many years. And, as much money as I made from my multiple streams of income (I've ALWAYS been great at calling large sums of money in), I somehow was ALWAYS on a rollercoaster of get it, save some, invest a bit, spend too much, deplete the savings, cash out the investments one by one, have nothing, then desperately wait for more to come in.

Why? Because no one had ever taught me the foundational wisdom for a GOOD life; no one ever taught me to **Pay Myself First**.

No one taught me to Choose ME, **every time**. No one told me that in order to live a truly happy, healthy, whole and fulfilling life, I had to **Put Me First**. So, I didn't.

I gave too much of my time, my belongings AND my money;
I allowed people far too much access to me;
I didn't say "No, that doesn't work for me";
I didn't learn how to properly utilise the tool that is money;
I didn't have a properly regulated nervous system and had little emotional control, so I talked too much and I lived in fight or flight mode, which means that **everything** became a battle;
I spent far too much time around people who weren't

headed anywhere and couldn't teach me anything or help me grow;

I allowed men and business associates to compromise me in various ways, because I couldn't speak up for myself;

I lost clients and contracts, because I created conflict when things were bothering me . . . .

Listen, just typing that list made me exhausted!

And, exhausted I was. I was also in victim mode a lot; financially broke far too much of the time; being disrespected by men in various ways; being used by friends, business associates and bad clients; swinging wildly between being effervescent and being discontent; sabotaging my own personal and professional progress and overall stagnant – because I was making the same mistakes over and over in my professional life, in relationships, and in how I treated myself.

Does any of that sound familiar to you? Can you see yourself in any of it, even just a tad? Because if yes, I'm here to tell you that it's time.

It is time to decide.

- Decide what **YOU actually want out of this life** – not what they told you, and not what is 'expected' for your age/ upbringing/ education/ job level.
- Decide what your **minimum requirements and standards** are for how you will be treated, how you will be spoken to, what you will be paid for your time and expertise, and for how you will live.
- Decide what your minimum **income requirement** is, and decide what your desired income is – no, the two are not the same. We're reaching for Thriving, not just barely surviving.
- Decide the **lifestyle/quality of life you wish to enjoy**: how do you most want to **feel** about and in

your life? What do your home, clothes, car and travel look and feel like? Vision Board it.

- Decide the **kind of people you want to have in your life**: create an avatar – what are their qualities and achievements, values + principles, income and quality of life?
- Decide the **impact you wish your business to make** in each client's life, in your community, and even in this world, then Vision Board it.
- Decide what **profit your business must make** monthly, quarterly and annually – they should differ, if you do proper financial planning for your business and a percentage of monthly and/or quarterly profit goes into income earning funds/accounts.
- Decide what you want each day to look like and more importantly, **feel like.**
- Decide **what makes you the most happy in your business**, what you can cut out or minimise, and how you can outsource the rest, now or bit by bit.
- Decide **what makes you the most happy in your life**, who and what you can cut out or minimise, and how you can outsource the rest, now or bit by bit.
- Decide that you CAN.
- Decide that you MUST.

Decide to Choose YOU, and to Pay Yourself First.

Of course, you can make all those decisions, write all those lists, and create the vision boards, but…. boundaries.

So, these are a few things you MUST practice saying in your mirror, and/or to your pet(s), until you can maintain cool, calm eye contact and say them to anyone (including your overbearing mother or aunt, and/or a ranting obnoxious client):

"That does not work for me, thanks".

"I'm sorry to hear that, but no thank you".

"Please stop what you're doing, it makes me very uncomfortable".

"If you continue down this path, we will have to end this conversation".

"Your investment is . . . (insert your high ticket amount here)".

"No thank you".

"Yes, I'd like that, please".

"May I have some of that?"

"How do I go about getting some of that / accessing that?"

"Is it possible to…. (make your request) please?"

"That does not work for me, but doing it this way would. (Go ahead and outline what works for you)".

"I don't feel equipped to make a decision in this moment. If you need an immediate answer then I understand, and I won't be able to participate".

"Please give me more information so that I can make a better decision".

"Sorry, my budget doesn't allow room for that right now".

"I would love to discuss that with you, but right now isn't a good time for me, sorry. Can we chat … (give day/time/etc)?"

"No, this is not up for negotiation".

"I need my team to be here, as I'm no longer comfortable discussing this one on one".

"I will need my lawyer present, before I can have that discussion".

"I totally get what you're saying, and unfortunately, as per our policies set out in the agreement, I'm unable to help with this; my hands are tied. What I **can** do for you though, is… (explain concessions you're willing to make)".

Of course, there are tons and tons of tough things to say in personal life and in business, but I tried to give you a good starting list.

. . .

If ANY of those caused you anxiety just by reading through them, then you KNOW you've got work to do this year!

And you know what? You can. Yep. Once you decide and commit, then it's game on.

Because really, who else is going to choose you, every time? Who else is going to bear the brunt if you continue failing yourself? Who else is going to continue living a less than life, because YOU won't put yourself first, Luv? Just you, right? And why? Because you're scared? Because it's hard? Because someone lied and told you that you couldn't? Balls!!! BALLS I say!!!!!

At the end of the day luv, in order to live that expanded, elevated, fulfilling, healthy, positively impactful life that you yearn so deeply for, you simply have to come around to the major and life altering lesson I had to learn:

In EVERY circumstance and in EVERY interaction, CHOOSE YOURSELF, and PAY YOURSELF FIRST.

BIO:

In 2011 VIP Life Success Coach KArima 'KAramel' Mckenzie-Thomas stepped into her Purpose of shifting people towards their best lives.Since then, the dynamic, creative, intuitive and life-altering Speaker and Writer, has become known, respected and sought after at home and internationally, for delivering her signature hard truths, different perspectives and no-nonsense tough love, that get people unstuck, inspired, and recommitted to themselves and their dreams.

You can find more of KArima's writing on Amazon in "The Make Me Good With Money Book" and in "Shine On You Crazy Daisy: Volume 3".

www.linktr.ee/teamviplife

23
JODEE-ENERGY

Jodee Peevor

What is the common overriding characteristic of you that people remark upon after leaving your presence? Mine is my "Jodee-Energy". I have a phenomenal natural energy, which, coupled with a heightened positivity and enthusiasm for life, is what I'm known for. I have heard innumerable times that my energy is uncommonly strong, and people seek it out - they say they need to visit to recharge. It is something I am incredibly proud of - even though it's not something I've consciously developed - as the song goes "Baby I was born this way".

I spent a long time being unsuccessfully "well behaved" - nearly four decades - before I truly embraced the effect of my gifts upon those around me. No more being "less" for those who were threatened by my energy, no more being small so they wouldn't feel smaller. I've even had a sister-in-law ask me to be "less". Can you picture the tears as they ran down my cheeks? I can still feel them now.

Running my own business has enabled me to be me. I don't

need to work with anyone who doesn't love my energy and enthusiasm. I really could only have been an entrepreneur! It's been an amazing journey to get here, and I still wake up every workday excited to start the day and jump on zoom with the team. So, let's go back to 2005 when it all started – ready?

Who was my very first client?

I had the most amazing home births with both of our children and in August 2005, 6 months after our first, Sam, was born, I was invited to run PR and Marketing for the company who manufactured the birthing pool we used. It was my dream job. I was so exhilarated from our birth and I naturally wanted to spread the word of how amazing a water birth is (whether at home, birthing centre or hospital.) In 2007 I realised I could take on more clients as Sam started nursery, so I registered as self-employed and became official! When my second client went through some financial difficulties, I decided to offer my assistant a job. I remember her first wage for the month was £60! At just 17 she was happy to grow her role as the business grew - thank you, Savannah, for having so much faith in me!! You have become my bestest ever friend and I thank my lucky stars we found each other. Within a few months Sav was full time and we began to grow our expertise and client base quickly from then on.

What was my first epiphany?

My joy came from creating gorgeous relationships with my clients and Savannah and I would spend time analysing when a project went south.

This was our first epiphany - learning that I had to create a stronger "dickhead filter" and not sign-up clients when my intuition shouted at me not to. In the early days you really do say yes to everyone who needs work doing and this is ok so long as it's a short-term thing, but you need to learn the profile of your ideal client sooner rather than later to truly grow your business with people who are full of joy to work with every day. Don't get me wrong, I still sign up the odd client who later turns out to be a mismatch, but I'm getting better and better at this. I ask myself "Would I like to friend this person on FB?" or "Would I invite this person home for dinner with my family". If the answers are no, this is my red flag. My intuition would also kick in, turning my stomach into butterflies and often I couldn't tell you why, but I just knew they weren't the client for me. Believe me, whenever I've ignored it, we've lived to regret it! It's ok that we're not suited to everyone, it's the same with friendships; finding your own inner radar is a huge part of your continued success (just don't beat yourself up if you miss the signs every now and again).

This "analysis" led us to recognise that the clients we really loved working with were those who wanted input from us; strategy support and marketing. We loved helping the client have impact, not just building their site for them. At the end of 2012 I was excited to start training as a Digital Marketer. I remember Valentine's Day 2013 when I first signed up for Ryan Deiss' Digital Marketer Lab - my husband Richard was sitting in the hotel suite at Coombe Abbey watching the rugby with beer in hand and I was on the huge four poster with afternoon tea (their scones are to die for) and my MAC as I worked through the trainings to understand funnel logic and customer journeys.

And my second epiphany?

Realising I didn't want to work with pain-point marketing was a breakthrough especially as I hadn't known that the opposite was possible! I kind of invented it on the spot because no one else was doing it back then. It was all what I call "negative marketing". Funnels that threatened to kill your grandmother and bury her under the patio if you didn't buy their course in the next 7 seconds – euuuggghhhhh!! Pain points – rub the salt in the wound – no no no!!

I wanted to work in positive marketing with heart centred entrepreneurs who wanted to create true impact in the world. Back then we'd only just started using that now over-used term which summed my ideal client up perfectly. They had soul and didn't just want to make money – they wanted reach and impact.

Facebook groups are where your people are

I was one of the first FB group marketers – I joined a massive online-guru's group in Autumn 2014 and realised there were hundreds of people in there who knew little to nothing about Wordpress or techy setup of funnels so I started helping them all answering their queries and helping them overcome their hurdles to keep them moving forward. People started asking to work with me as their business coach and imple-menter. I had no idea that me just showing up and helping people would actually grow my business too! I didn't start doing it for that reason and was overwhelmed by the effect. I tripled my business in 6 weeks from Feb that year. It was exhilarating! That summer we incorporated our second limited company and named it "Online and Totally Fabulous Ltd".

My biggest, most painful serendipitous lesson in my whole business journey

Behind the scenes, the "online guru" was planning a big period of growth and was actually going to start offering "done for you" services to her members – so whilst I had, up until now, been an asset to her by supporting her members for free, I overnight turned into a competitor. I woke up on the morning of our dear friends' wedding to find I couldn't access the group and my membership had been refunded. Ouch! No email or message to explain. I felt sick! I felt like my income source had disappeared overnight! We drove to the wedding with me in shock. Goodness me!

What a terribly painful lesson. I realised my next group relationship had to be very different. I would be a valued, supported and encouraged member of their support team and would make sure I had the full permission of the group leaders to support their members in tech and setup issues.

The Universe had my back

Invited by other members of the "online guru's" group to build their event website and be one of their speakers proved that these relationships hadn't disappeared because I wasn't in the group anymore – not even slightly! People started reaching out to DM me despite me not being in the group. My business actually began to grow more!

My next beautifully timed meeting was with the lovely David Vox at an event and he turned me onto Kajabi. I became a founder member of New Kajabi that Spring. I was instantly so valued and appreciated for my help in the group and in early 2018 I was invited alongside 6 others to become official Kajabi Ambassadors and play a recognised role in the group with trainings for members and moderator status. I felt seen and respected, and my business continued to grow as I embraced this new platform. The developers asked for details of the funnels I wanted to build and they created the frameworks and functionality to support them by the end of that first summer! What a company! I was proud and thankful to have found my space.

. . .

The team – oh what a team!

Savannah and I brought on an amazing young 20 year old – the son of our business photographer Abby. He desperately needed a change of direction having hated recruitment and was excited to join as an intern. The interview turned into an offer of a fulltime position! I said, "Jack, can you video edit?" he said "No, but I'm keen to learn!" – and kaboom, our second fulltime member of staff joined the team. This was May 2019. I started to grow the team more quickly from that Christmas. I realised that a lot of people had extra things that brought them joy and if I was the kind of leader who enabled them to do both, they would be the happiest people ever! Amy joined us New Year 2020 and works with us around her Midwifery degree. Savannah is working in A&E and studying for her nursing degree whilst working for us. Jiska is off to the Seychelles to support marine conservation for 3 months. Holly is training to be a Primary School teacher and my nephew Luke is studying for a Psychology degree – both of whom were previously in soul destroying roles in retail and recruitment and so relieved to move forward with this gorgeously friendly team. Nicola works in Conveyancing alongside our work and Michele has her own private clients. Even my husband Richard was able to retire in October 2019 and is running his own street food business.

I've also got to thank Covid – you've got to love Serendipity! My darling brother who lives in Sydney and is an actor and director was stuck in his one bedroom flat bored out of his mind during the first lockdown in April 2020! I said "Hey you! Fancy joining the team" He said "OMG yes! Can I still accept acting parts when I want to and what will I do in the team?" I said "Of course you can! That's how we work – and I don't know – we'll figure it out!" What utter joy! We quickly developed the Creative Director role for him as he thrived as our voice and performance coach for our client's marketing video creation. During 2021 we brought onboard a fulltime assistant for him who is also super excited to be able to accept acting roles and work with the team around those commitments.

As the team grew, I realised that our keyword was "Joy" – once a week I ask each team member if they are "working in their joy", if not, we redistribute the tasks or I hire someone new to do them. I also ask if any clients are "heavy" – and if they are and I can't turn it around, I fire the client. My team feels heard and seen and they get to work 100% in their joy. Oh and we only work a 32 hour, 4 day week and every quarter we all get a week off plus 3 weeks off at Christmas and twice yearly Cherie comes to office and everyone has full body massages – kaboom!

We're all super excited for our future together – the team is now 12 and it's the perfect dynamic!

Thank you for listening to my journey!

BIO:

I'm Jodee, I'm a marketing specialist with golden energy whose team specialises in all the wondrous tech and digital mastery needed to build amazing online businesses that fly. We are a team of 12 based in England and Australia. We build businesses with Kajabi, Wordpress & Joomla running advertising campaigns to optimise the funnels we build for our clients. We support heart centred businesses with all the tools and techniques that I have developed since 2005 running my wonderful marketing agency.

www.jodeepeevor.com

24
THE INTROVERT REBEL

Ilga Becker

I don't like hierarchies and I like working by my own rules. You might think that qualifies me to be an entrepreneur but the path to feeling comfortable in my self-employment has been a rocky one.As a child, I was both shy and rebellious. I hated drawing attention to myself and yet, I wasn't afraid to stand out when trends didn't feel right to me. Being very introverted and thriving on alone time, I enjoyed the few days I got to work from home in the job I had as a student. Part of my job involved working with startups and it sparked my dream of running my own business - one day. In fact, when I tested a game my employer developed for university students who wanted to start their own business, I scored highly. The dream of being my own boss was born but I never would have dared to go for it. I was sure you needed to be much more extroverted to be able to sell yourself and I believed I lacked the experience I needed to succeed on my own. As a consequence I applied for a job and worked in an agency for almost two years, gaining a lot of experience not just in SEO itself, but also in how to deal with clients and what to offer. Then I felt I needed a new challenge and I quit my job, the dream of going freelance or self-employed emerged again. It wasn't before I was unable to find a new better suited job in the short timeframe I had, that I even considered giving it a try. I found my first client through a former coworker and decided I would see it as an experiment: do I have what it takes to be self-employed? How do I deal with the insecurity, can I motivate myself and how hard will it be to find new clients? I gave myself a few months to test my new work situation - and realised it is just what I want to do!

After deciding that, it does indeed feel good to be my own boss and set my own schedule (within limits), I had my first logo created, my website built and booked my first professional photo shoot for my new website. I didn't know any other entrepreneurs, I had no mentor or coach so the only experience I could draw from was the corporate world. To me, professional meant corporate so corporate I went. All the service providers I worked with were very professional and provided exactly what I asked of them. I ended up with a rather boring corporate looking website and plain logo that didn't really represent me but did their job.

The photoshoot resulted in very corporate looking photos in a shiny dark blue blazer (because I felt that's what you had to look like if you work in online marketing) with metal and glass in the background and some typical "boss poses". I tamed my hair and took off my spider necklace that I would normally wear 24/7. Friends were amused by these photos, but there was no-one who told me I might have gone wrong because my friends didn't know anything about running your own business.

I did business in a similar way: using what I had learned in my agency days, making sure I looked corporate when meeting clients. One meeting in particular served as an eye-opener in hindsight. I met a potential new client who had shown interest in working with me. We met in a pretty posh restaurant that they had chosen, I showed up wearing a blazer, suit pants - and my Doc Martens because that helped me still feel a little bit like myself. Since I never wear formal clothes in real life, I felt like I had dressed up for a role that didn't really suit me. The meeting was stiff and awkward and it didn't come as a surprise that I wasn't hired.

Little by little I began to rebel against the dress code that was mostly in my mind. I was so afraid of failing and making mistakes that I followed the rules I had made up myself - even though the rebel in me absolutely hated it. I started wearing more casual clothes in client meetings, even showing tattoos when I felt comfortable enough. I started to feel that both my website and my photos didn't represent me at all, I wanted to give both clients and prospects a better idea of who I really am.

I booked another photoshoot with a different agenda. My idea was to tone down who I was so that I wouldn't repel clients but I also didn't want to look too corporate anymore. We ended up shooting with plain concrete walls in the background, me wearing either a plain blue or black long sleeve shirt and my spider necklace. Tattoos stayed hidden in most of them, except for a few "rockstar photos" in a black t-shirt that I wasn't sure I would use. The result felt more "me" - but a boring version of myself. That was my new idea of "professional" - now showing too much personality when you are a bit different from many experts in my industry.

The new website and logo used my old corporate colours and still looked very clean but also a lot more creative than the version before. The logo uses my handwriting and there are all these fun little details that look a lot more playful and less corporate, yet still professional.

A lot of progress both in my mindset and marketing assets and yet I didn't feel 100% comfortable with what I represented. I still felt like I had suppressed so much of myself. I started doing work a little differently and would show up way more authentically with clients and prospects and it felt a lot more aligned. I started to get booked out, too, so it paid off.

When I went to Italy for a business retreat and one of the brilliant women taking part was a photographer, we used the chance for a business photoshoot in the breathtaking scenery of Matera. We went for three different types of photos, representing the different sides in me: Casual Goth, Rockabilly and Gothy Witch. For the last ones we even used props like a crystal ball or a wand to refine my branding.

I had started using the term "SEO Witch" that had naturally evolved over a few years since a friend had called me that in German ("SEO Hexe") and I realised that it is a title that people remember and one that feels very much "me". Of course my new photos had to reflect that.

When the photos were done and I showed them to friends, side by side with the photos from the first two shoots, I got a lot of positive responses. Finally I had photos that represented me well and that showed my personality. One of the comments I got was that I looked very comfortable and natural. Finally there was no more repressing sides of myself, no more toning down or dressing up.

In daily life I started to own the term "SEO Witch" a little more every day. I put it as a title in business networks, used it on clients' Slack channels and introduced myself with it. I was still careful about not being "too much" in client calls or meetings but I slowly started to be more daring when I felt I could get away with it. Glittery lipstick, dark makeup, metal band shirts.

Being more authentic and hiding fewer sides of me led to some amazing connections. The client call where we talked about fantasy books and favourite Spanish football teams. The meeting in a very stiff atmosphere where the very corporate looking client and I found out that we like the same bands and have been to the same annual Goth event. Clients have complimented me on fancy lipsticks and Gothy looks. So far there has been no negative response - unless they didn't tell me. Instead there have been deeper connections and my business is going better than ever.

And the worries about being too introverted to "sell myself"? I learned that introverts have their strengths too and can be amazing business people. If you have a good network of people (forming close connections has been one of my strengths), you don't necessarily have to sell yourself actively. Until today, I have never cold called anyone, the only sales calls were ones with people who were already interested. Another strength? Being a good listener and asking the right questions. A genuine interest in people and solving their problems. Pair this with authenticity and it attracts the right people.

These days, I question everything I used to believe about running your own business. How you have to work. Who you need to be. How you have to look. Almost all of them have been proven wrong over the years - or at least optional and I decided to opt out of them. It is entirely possible to be successful in business, even if you are an introvert rebel!

BIO:

Ilga Becker, the SEO Witch, has been helping businesses increase their traffic with fun SEO training and non-overwhelming consulting for over a decade. She is passionate about simplifying complex topics like technical SEO and believes in imagination and individuality instead of rules that are set in stone. Privately, Ilga loves her squirrel friends, reading fantasy books, going to Metalcore gigs and dancing to Dark Electro or Rockabilly.

www.ilwen.com

25

AN AUDIENCE WITH VICTORIA

Victoria Schofield

I was delighted to be asked to write a chapter for Volume 4 of this wonderful set of books. I was Chapter 27 of Volume 2, "Too Many Strawberries In The Jam". Page 170, according to my Darling Dad. Brush past him and he will give you a copy! I think he is keeping Amazon solvent! However, when I agreed to contribute again I wondered whether I actually had anything further to offer that would be useful.

So, I came up with this idea. A Q-and-A session. People I know from all different backgrounds asking me about running an independent business.

So...

How did you know where to begin and what to do?

The concept of The Cup and Saucer ("TCAS") was always a very simple one so I think that helps with where to begin. Nice tea cups and saucers, lovely plates, cakes, scones, cream, jam, sandwiches, linen napkins, then deliver Afternoon Tea as a beautifully presented gift. That was the easy bit. The rest of what to do was done in stages. Researching what other people were or were not doing around the country with the same idea was a priority. Not many at all and only one in my area in fact. Now, that was crucial as this discovery either limited the competition or indicated that there wasn't a need. Then the practical bit. I read so much about starting up your own business as everything is available online. However, I am not talking about weeks of it. I just sat down and over the course of two days had learnt a bit about what you needed to do to start your own Small Business. That is actually a term I do not like - "Small Business". I am an Independent Business, small yet beautiful, but one day it could be great yet beautiful. I found this amazing course, simply by looking on the web for "support for new businesses". It was free to starter Independent Businesses that gave me online weekly seminars, a mentor, access to resources and support. Invaluable, as I could listen to other people's experiences as well. However, a lot of it was just common sense and exceptionally good luck if I am perfectly honest.

What was your greatest fear when you started that business and what was the reality of that fear?

Failure. Pure and simple and it still haunts me now as much as it did in the early days. I can still wake up in a blind panic and then spend the rest of the morning, with staggeringly dramatic effect, announcing to the very long-suffering Mr. Schofield that I should never have thought that this would a good idea, I was mad, I need to go back and find a regular job. He just nods and almost without exception on days like this I get a couple of orders in and I start strutting about telling him he had no reason to doubt me. It is a natural human reaction to doubt yourself and it is very much one of your worst enemies in this game, but you just have to shake it off and keep going. Otherwise, you give into the fear and it wins, when it should not.

How have you managed to juggle your work life, your family life and your social life to maintain a healthy work life balance?

I was hopeless at first. An absolute nightmare. I don't think we ate for about two weeks! I felt I had to be on the computer or my phone all of the time just trying to set everything up, creating posts for social media, checking the emails every 5 minutes in case I got an order in. Baking for the photo shoots, completing all the paperwork. Once it was up and running, I calmed a bit but not entirely. In the end the decision was made that there was actually no such thing as "An Afternoon Tea Emergency" so I stopped checking emails in bed. I implemented stop times and start times. Whilst it is my business and I want the business, no one will die if an order they place at midnight for a cream tea is not responded to until the next morning. I think the crazy early days were made easier because Mr. Schofield was working from home, so just having the company there helped immensely in terms of a work life balance because we could have lunch together and a cup of tea together. I am now quite good and my family and friends understand that I have to work odd hours and I have to work weekends and that is just the nature of the beast. I still get it wrong sometimes when I should prioritise it better, but I keep trying.

Going into business by yourself is a very courageous and bold move. What was the biggest challenge about sole working/management and how did you combat it?

The hardest thing was the sense of "you really are on your own, Victoria". Initially I didn't have anyone that close that I could ask about what to do next. In my previous life if I had a problem I could wander into someone else's office and say "What do you think about this?" Or pick up the phone and say "Can you come and look at this as I am really not sure about it". We all would pick each other's brains to find a solution. Whilst my family and friends would allow their brains to be picked, they didn't have knowledge of setting up or running a business, and to be fair I think some of them were in shock that I could bake! So, I found online groups. I joined them. I read all of their blogs and watched how they asked questions and was over-whelmed by the amazingly intelligent and professional responses they received. I eventually plucked up the courage to introduce myself and offer opinions if I thought they would help. In time, if I got stuck, I would ask for help and seek advice to which I always received superb and much needed guidance and support so that took me out of "sole working" as it were. It was a network. It was actually The Hampshire Women's Business Group that were very instrumental in this and it is Trudy Simmons, the founder of that group, who is the force behind these books and for that I will be eternally grateful. So, I think you have to force yourself out of the shade and into the light to understand that you actually have support and you are not working alone but you do need to actively go looking for it.

Do you still have the confidence in the business as we come out of lockdown?

TCAS was born in lockdown for the very purpose of helping people let others, that they could not get to, know that they were loved and thought of. So, in light of that simple concept, I do have confidence in the business. In the same way that any Independent Business should. A release from lockdown will not alter the fact that we cannot be with family and friends all of the time. If there is a good quality product and a need for it just keep going. Hold on. Promote the life out of it.

If you could go back in time before you started the business and give yourself one piece of advice, what would it be?

There are a few answers I could pick with this one but I think the most important and arguably the simplest is to have faith in yourself and in your product. Simply because if we don't, nobody else will. It is easier said than done without a shadow of a doubt because you are putting yourself out there saying "look at me, I am fantastic, my product is great, please do buy it" even when you have no idea if it will work. My experience shows that it will if you believe in yourself, your product and your brand. It is your name on it so you must have faith. You actually owe it to yourself to have the hope and the well-deserved confidence in your product.

How will your business evolve in the next five years?

A brilliant question and something that every new Independent Business Owner should consider but I suspect, like me, hasn't quite got round to it yet. However, I am going to be brutally honest and say that I really do not know. I know that I will continue to strive for it to be a success but that is a given for all of us. The possibility of franchises has crossed my mind. I would love to do more event catering but I am still an acorn just beginning to realise it may just be an Oak Tree one day. I think to get to the bottom of where I would like to go with TCAS I need to get some professional business project management guidance.

.   .   .

You were a commercial contract litigation solicitor for years. DO you miss your old life?

I do not miss my "old life" at all. That is the truth. I am an incredibly lucky person and I have a wonderful life. Yes, it is very different but that doesn't bother me. In an odd way I feel more secure, in control and confident than I have in years. I have a fantastic husband, family and friends which obviously makes it a lot easier but I also have a tremendous amount of pride that I have created TCAS. It is my business, I have worked for it, I continue to work for it and starting TCAS has afforded me the opportunity to stand back and say "I did that and it is a little bit fabulous".

I am fascinated about what I have learned through this process of being asked the questions I would not probably have asked myself. Maybe because the question hadn't occurred to me. Possibly, and slightly more likely, because if I had asked the question, I would have been afraid of the answer. I would encourage you to look at the questions and adapt them to your story, your business, your journey. Ask your own questions. Get others to ask them of you if you like. There are no wrong answers at all but make sure the ones you give yourself are honest.

In Volume 2 I wrote "Learn everything that you can before you start". (Dad says it is page 173, halfway down, FYI). I stand by that but you have to keep learning about your own goals, your own plans, your strengths, your weaknesses and your abilities as they will change as you get used to doing what it is you set out to do. It's not easy and I will not do it as regularly as I should but it is, nonetheless, worth doing.

Anyway, I hope this helps.

Many, many thanks to everyone who has supported TCAS. I am so grateful.

This chapter is dedicated to my Mum, Susan, a connoisseur

of Afternoon Tea. She set the bar very high. So, with love and thanks to her. x

BIO:

Victoria is the founder and owner of The Cup and Saucer, an Afternoon Tea Delivery service.

She is 43, from Sunderland and has lived in Winchester for 9 years. She lived in London for 17 years and was a Litigation Solicitor. She is married to Marc and owns Margot the dog.

She loves travelling, baking, reading and people, fascinating creatures.

www.thecupandsaucer.com

26
FROM STRESSED TO SERENE
(THE HARD WAY)

Helen Davis

I never exactly *decided* to start a business. Working for myself wasn't a long-term dream. Rather, when my entire life imploded, I gradually began to understand that there was no going back. If I was ever going to be happy and healthy, I had instead to move forward and create an entirely new life for myself.

A life that didn't revolve around endless deadlines and making money for other people.

A life where I had space to breathe.

If I'd realised at the time how completely and utterly I'd be turning everything I knew upside down, I might not have had the courage to go through with it... but then again, I never really felt like I had any choice.

Living the dream

In early 2012 I turned 46. From the outside, it probably looked as if my life was perfect. A successful business analyst with a well-established niche and an international reputation, I was married, child-free by choice, and living in a four-bedroom house in the Hampshire countryside. Despite managing a team, I worked mainly from home, travelling to London once a week and internationally several times a year. We enjoyed regular holidays; weekends were spent entertaining or visiting friends, walking our dog and riding a friend's horse. Sure, when any of my friends were asked to describe me, "stressed" was the first word that sprang to mind, but that's normal, right? In fact, underneath this idyllic exterior – and unbeknown to me or anyone around me – I was spiralling into crisis. Twenty years into my career, I knew it wasn't my dream job but still had no idea "what I want to do when I grow up". When the boutique consultancy firm I'd helped build was acquired by a huge multi-national in 2010, it triggered a life-long and deeply rooted fear of change. The smallest mistake or slightest criticism plunged me into paroxysms of self-doubt, leaving me tearful and unable to focus. I found it almost impossible to think positively. My physical health was deteriorating too: chronic migraines and frequent throat infections meant I was over-reliant on strong medication. Working remotely meant I could hide my increasing fragility from colleagues, but at home my marriage was suffering. In March 2012, shortly before the biggest event of my working year, I was struck down by a flu-like virus. I grudgingly took to my bed, expecting to be back at my desk within days. Instead, a week later I found myself in a state of total physical and emotional collapse, barely able to function and spending up to 23 hours a day in bed. Over four decades of low-level anxiety, stress and insecurity had finally taken their toll. A diagnosis of ME/CFS confirmed it: I was officially burnt out.

System reboot required

For the first few weeks I did little more than sleep fitfully. My body was drained of all energy, like a spent battery. My limbs felt strangely disconnected from my torso. Taking a shower or negotiating the stairs was a major undertaking that required planning beforehand and rest afterwards. A life-long bookworm, I could barely concentrate on the radio, let alone read. As the weeks turned into months and I began to spend more time out of bed, the realisation slowly dawned that I would not be going back to work any time soon. Along with huge amounts of guilt about letting down my colleagues, I began to feel something else: a growing sense of relief. A glimmer of hope that maybe, just maybe, there was a way out. That perhaps *this* was the breathing space I'd been longing for. And as I finally allowed myself to open up to the possibility of change, the people who could help me began to show up in my life.First was a highly skilled Bowen Therapy practitioner who had been treating the rest of my family for years – but not me, because I'd always been "too busy". Through her came a dentist who began treating the TMJ (jaw) issues that were exacerbating my migraines. He in turn referred me to two "outstanding" practitioners: a hypnotherapist and an osteopath. Meanwhile I began attending therapeutic yoga classes, where my exhausted body and mind were finally given permission to rest.

With my support team in place, at last my healing could begin.

While the body work and yoga gently and subtly began to make space in my tense, exhausted body, hypnotherapy helped me, for the first time in my life, to explore what was going on in my own mind.

It was a revelation.

Rebuilding from the ground up

Over the next five years, with the love and support of family, friends and health professionals, I gradually rebuilt my life. Key to this process was understanding how I'd ended up in this state. How, despite my conventionally happy childhood, my deep-rooted need for approval had led to decades of trying to keep everyone around me happy, trying to mould myself into the person that (I thought) they wanted me to be. How my profound fear of change had kept me locked into old, familiar patterns, until I had worn away my own sense of self so completely that I no longer had any idea who I was or what I wanted.

Thanks to my illness, I'd already had to let go of all the physical things I'd been doing to keep myself busy, but that was just the start. Despite the almost constant brain fog, convincing my mind that it was ok sometimes to be still, to rest, took a long time. To be honest, I'm still working on it!

Meanwhile, the gentle yet deep practice of Scaravelli-inspired yoga taught me to start *listening* to my body rather than telling it what to do, gradually unlocking the tension I'd been holding in my limbs for decades, making space for movement. I am not naturally bendy (in fact, if you'd told me a few years ago that I'd end up teaching yoga I'd have laughed in your face!). But today my 56-year-old body is more flexible than it has ever been. And with each new physical release has come a corresponding emotional release, sometimes subtle, sometimes surprisingly profound. Because, as my yoga teacher memorably told me, "Where there's space, there's healing."

Meanwhile working with a skilled hypnotherapist helped me uncover and address the deep-held beliefs that (without my even realising it) had been determining how I thought and behaved in any given situation my whole life. With her support I was able not only to transform my own internal landscape, but to make space for an entirely new worldview, one that allows me to live my life in genuine gratitude for everything that has brought me to this point (yes, even my illness!). And which, in turn, opened my heart to the timeless wisdom of yoga philosophy and meditation.

And as my approach to life evolved, so, inevitably, did my circumstances. Over this five-year period I let go of the career that had defined me, accepted that my marriage had run its course and relocated to a new town. In fact, other than my family, the only constant in my life was my beloved patterdale terrier, Muppet!

And somewhere along the line, I finally realised what I wanted to do when I grew up.

I wanted to be a hypnotherapist.

And a yoga teacher.

Making it happen

In 2014 I started my hypnotherapy training. Sitting in class that first day I was suddenly overwhelmed by an unfamiliar feeling. I knew, without a shadow of doubt, that I was exactly where I was meant to be. And I knew that I had never, ever felt that way before. The three years of yoga teacher training that followed only served to deepen this new sense of certainty.

Today, my life has changed beyond recognition, not only externally but – much more importantly – internally. I had to hit rock bottom before I was ready to listen to what my body and mind had been trying to tell me for years. The combination of yoga and hypnotherapy transformed my life. It revealed an inner strength that had previously eluded me and provided a blueprint for accessing the wellspring of peace that exists deep inside every one of us. It enabled me to shift my default state from stressed, to serene.

I'm now passionate about helping others make the changes they need to make *before* they reach burnout, rather than afterwards, whether on the yoga mat or in the hypnotherapy chair.

And then came 2020, and the world changed overnight.

In mid-March, as Lockdown loomed, I took my business online. I already had a few overseas hypnotherapy clients, so knew how effective that aspect of my work could be on-screen, but yoga was a different matter. To be honest, I'd always been very dismissive of online yoga, both as a student and as a teacher. How wrong I was!

From that very first class it became clear that the energetic connection that we create when we practice together has nothing to do with physical proximity. We can be just as connected on Zoom. And it turns out that there are many benefits to practicing together, remotely. The gentle, yet deep, yoga that I teach is ideally suited to practicing in one's own home. My ability to explain verbally exactly how I'm inviting my students to ease into each pose, means they can relax and let my voice guide them through movement and stillness.

In fact, it works so well that in January 2021 I officially moved my weekly classes online, allowing me to open them up to students outside my local area. I also run regular in-person workshops, giving those who want to practice with me face-to-face the opportunity to step away from their busy lives for a few hours and make space for movement, stillness and deep, deep rest.

Taking stock

This year, 2022, marks two major anniversaries for me: 10 years since I became ill (March) and five since I started my business (May). I can honestly say that I am both immensely proud of what I have achieved and frustrated that I have not yet achieved more!

I consider myself "recovered" from ME/CFS, although I still have to pace myself. Overdoing things usually leads to being floored by a three-day migraine. These are both deeply annoying and intensely painful – and yet I am grateful to them. For it is these migraines that have prevented me from experiencing the constant relapses that characterise ME/CFS for so many people.

This in-built "early warning system" means that I cannot work the hours that so many small business owners do. My business is definitely a tortoise, rather than a hare! And that's ok. Because I'm still here. I'm still taking One Step Forward each day and, equally importantly, helping my clients do the same thing.

One big advantage of taking things slowly is that I've had time to really think about where I'm going. And over the past few months something exciting has been brewing. A project that brings together everything I've learned over the past decade. One that will allow me to work directly with the clients that I'm best placed to help, wherever they live. Supporting and guiding them, as they discover their own path from stressed to serene, one step at a time.

So, what more is there to say but… watch this space!

BIO:

Helen Davis is the founder of One Step Forward. Drawing on her training in clinical hypnotherapy, yoga and meditation she helps busy people make space – physically, mentally and emotionally. Space to breathe. Space to be. Space to learn who they really are. Because where there's space, there's healing. Having learned the hard way what happens when we ignore the warning signs, Helen is passionate about helping women who work for themselves learn to listen to their body and make space in their lives, BEFORE they burn out.

www.onestepforward.today

27
BUILDING RELATIONAL CAPITAL

Heather Barrie

I f "roller-coastery" were a word – it would be the word that
describes my entrepreneurial journey - from hair-raising,
scream-out-loud moments to the slow climb, filled with excited
yet fearful anticipation - I've been through it all!

But it's important for me to head back a few years, just a
few. I was born in London in the 1960s with a serious heart
problem, to parents who were usually resident in South Africa. I
am eternally grateful for the team at Charing Cross Hospital,
for without those awesome people (and my parents' incredible
love), I would not have survived my traumatic first seven
months in this world. The reason I mention this is that the
energy of that will to survive and thrive, together with the right
people around me to support my journey, have been crucial to
my journey. But these realisations have only come to me
recently.

We returned to Africa and shortly after successful cardiac
surgery when I was five, I just got on with my very young life.
Not much got in my way and even though the medics told me

that I had to be super-cautious, my folks were not the molly-coddling types and I was free to do pretty much as I wanted, so long as I didn't do any long distance running. (What?? I was five - and who likes long distance running anyway!?)

I also set up my first business when I was five (it was a big year!). I ran it with my sister –"J&H Chickens". We got the eggs from the family chickens (Dad paid for the chickens, their feed and their upkeep) and we then sold them to my mum and the neighbours! In effect, Dad paid for the eggs twice, but it was our first enterprise and the eggs were delicious!

School, hockey, piano lessons, lots of sunshine and growing up (well – getting older – not entirely sure I've ever grown up) then got in the way of any teenage entrepreneurship. But I always had an eye for a bargain, made sure my change was correct in every transaction, and had side hustle jobs from the age of 15.

I saved like a demon because in my heart, I knew I wanted an adventure and I knew that I wanted to live in Europe. I'm definitely a northern hemisphere, European kinda gal! I had so many interests and paths that I could take that I struggled to decide on my university direction. In the end, I plumped for the safe option – with hindsight – the safe, yet really "not me", option! I opted for an auditing degree – I was thinking about the money I would earn when I got that fab graduate job. I switched focus midway to management accounts and business economics – I can tell, you're bored already – I was! But I kept going and graduated at 20 and then a month after my 21st birthday, with all my savings from all those side hustles, I packed up my briefcase (ok – I had studied accountancy and it was the yuppie 1980s!), flew north and dived into work!!

But full-time corporate life was not for me (I last did that nine-to-five thing in my 20s) and I also quickly realised that, although good at it, accountancy just didn't make my heart sing! I started to study other things, including shiatsu and sports nutrition. I set up my first UK business in 1992 – office-based massage based on shiatsu. I was a ground-breaker – the first person to do this style of stress management in offices in the West End. As there wasn't any social media, mobile phones, or influencers to say how wonderful it was, I did it the old-fashioned way. I found medium-sized creative and tech businesses with forward-thinking HR managers and leaders – I wrote to them and followed them up with a phone call from the red phonebox at the end of the road!

Some liked the idea and were open to a free trial. I picked up three clients in a few months: a software house, a publisher and a group of venture capitalists. It was cash-in-hand (all declared of course as I was saving for a mortgage!) but somewhat unpredictable, as income depended on who was in the office when I was there, or whether an in-house crisis prevented anyone from pitching up at all! But I buzzed around London on my moped with a fancy treatment mat on my back and gradually my reputation and bank balance grew.

But in all honesty – despite working with super interesting and lovely clients and doing something I loved - I couldn't do enough hours to generate the income that I wanted and wasn't keen to take on other people and manage them. So I picked up some part-time, well paid accountancy work and the stress management continued as a fun side hustle.

The lucrative work then rather took over for a few years and the hustle diminished to a whimper. But gradually, the nagging feeling that I really didn't enjoy accountancy or the corporate world returned, together with the lure of doing my own thing. This coincided with being made redundant and the decision to move to the south coast. A perfect time for self-employment once more!

I decided to resurrect the stress management business but aimed at training and inspiring entrepreneurs to look after their health. After all, if these self-starters aren't able to perform to their best, then their businesses couldn't operate optimally.

I was excited for this new venture. I had some small savings (although I really did also want a new kitchen in my new home!), so I used the same low-cost tactics as I had in London and I quickly picked up my first client – I thought I'd struck gold! But that's all it ever was – one great client, and they only wanted two projects. But I kept on marketing and ignored my intuition that it wasn't the right offer: networking, changing my name, changing my offer, printing more flyers. But the business didn't fly! So I had to get a badly paid job – back in accountancy and I licked my wounds. But not for long though, as being in Sussex was reigniting the entrepreneurial energy I had had as a five-year-old – that just do it, that JFDI!

I needed a total change and I went left-field. Inspired by time in Seattle and the growing café culture in the UK, I decided to do what no sane person should do: I invested in a crazy French truck with a coffee bar in its boot, started negotiating with Southern Railway (again, something that no sane person should do) and set up a coffee bar outside Arundel station, serving early morning commuters. I embarked on my journey into the wonderful world of coffee entrepreneurship. The hours were awful, the weather was challenging and the train service erratic. However, my 10 years of 4.40am alarms, snow, ice, heatwaves and rain (so much rain), were made a joy by the people I served and the joy that I could bring them. Dispensing awesome coffee to grateful commuters was the best job in the world. It brought together my favourite things – people, business and hospitality.

The income wasn't great, as I was at a small station, but my soul was on cloud nine. I'd discovered two of the three aspects of Ikigai – that sweet spot of doing what you love, doing what people want and being paid what you need from it. I was almost there. I started to find other events to boost the coffers and started to explore the idea of franchising – surely the most logical way to build a coffee empire. But that gremlin from my stress management days raised its charming little head again. I didn't want to be managing people, and the people I would have taken on would surely have the wherewithal to set up their own show!

I was getting restless. How was I to progress from that point? I bought my coffee supplier's business and made the roast my own (it's great having your name on the label!). I started consulting for people who wanted to create their own mobile coffee bars. I had lashings of credibility – eight years in mobile coffee, 200,000 coffees made, an accountancy background – I had a unique offer. This business started to grow, so when the rail strikes of 2016/17 started to take their toll on my station business and my patience, I knew it was time to hang up my station kiosk keys! I handed my pitch to a friend and focused on the wholesale and consultancy business (with a little bit of politics on the side – but running for parliament is a story for another book)!

I was building a great reputation for my creativity and my tasty coffee, and had great relationships with my suppliers and customers. However, sadly, that counted for very little when Covid hit. I'd been focusing my coffee machine marketing on encouraging people in offices to use coffee as a way to bring people together in creative conversation at work – like they do in Sweden, where they have a daily break for coffee, cake and conversation called Fika. But as we went into lockdown, no one was getting together with anyone and most of my clients were forced to close, albeit temporarily.

I needed a new business and I needed it fast! I connected with my friend Richard – we'd been introduced a few years beforehand and had often chatted through business ideas. Lockdown 2020 was the time to take action! I've been networking actively for many years and I'm very aware of how networks and building relational capital are the basis for all great business successes. So within a week of the doors closing around us, we had a long chat about how we could bring together our networks in Sussex and Yorkshire and our extensive LinkedIn connections!

Within the month we hosted our first event, which was a success. Our instinct that Richard and I would be a good partnership was right. We have a great working chemistry, a balance of skills and two cheeky smiles, and made a corking £124.80 for our first event. We were excited and inspired to see how the next event would go, and we've pretty much held at least one event every week since. Our niche would be working with owner-run, entrepreneurial businesses and we wanted to focus on learning, LinkedIn and on supporting people who are great at what they do to achieve their dreams – it was much more than a networking business. There are other coaches and networking groups out there, but with our experience and emphasis on active learning and community support, we knew that ours was innovative and that it delivered something different.

We've had two name changes but one thing is for sure, we've created something unique. For me, I've finally trusted my intuition and it's the culmination of all those years of searching for something that really unites my passions, together with an offer that people want, and it's growing! I've found my Ikigai - I get to inspire others, I get to be "on stage" and work with incredible entrepreneurs who love what we do and who give back to us in equal measure. And I get to share this with a wonderful business partner – perhaps that was the missing ingredient all along!

BIO:

Effective Entrepreneurs does what it says on the tin. We're an online support platform for owner-run businesses who are brilliant at what they do but who miss that sense of team camaraderie, that accountability, that potential to bounce ideas and learn from others – it's often lacking in the exciting but potentially lonely entrepreneurial world. We lean in, learn from each other and have just launched our unique online co-working space. Please come and visit and see how your solopreneur's journey doesn't need to be a solo journey!

https://linktr.ee/heatherbarrie

28

HOW TO RISE AND THRIVE IN CHALLENGING TIMES

Raimonda Jankunaite

W hen we set out into the year 2020 most people thought it would be a turning point into a whole new chapter. A more positive, successful and truly transformational year. It was a year to go for our big 'now or never' goals. For me it was a year of expansion. Up to that point I had already hosted some very successful events in London for Women in Business Club and it was a year for us to take things global.

We had already attracted some international speakers and guests to our events and our community were asking us when we were planning on hosting events internationally. So, 2020 was the year for us to take our events to the USA - first stop being Atlanta Georgia, with NYC, Los Angeles, Toronto Canada, Ibiza Spain, and London to follow. I started to plan and research for our first event in March for Atlanta, from carefully selecting the event venue, interviewing vendors and confirming hand selected speakers.

Right at the beginning of planning for this event, I only knew one person there, Michelle Enjoli who was a speaker at our London event the year before. By the end of month two our database increased with more than 2,000 people from Atlanta, the top 3rd city for our social media audience was Atlanta and so we had the buzz going for this event. Women started to book their tickets, flights and accommodations. Speakers and attendees were preparing to fly from across the USA and the UK to be there. We had a venue of 250 people and 8 speakers lined up ready, and with the expectations from events in Atlanta being pretty high, it was set to be one of our biggest yet, and probably most extravagant events to date.

As the new year started, we began to see the news of the CoronaVirus spreading rapidly. It was going from some distant virus in China to fast approaching in the UK, Europe and the world. Every day the cases were rising and people's worries became more evident. Our ticket sales slowed right down, and we were all watching in anticipation of what would happen. I recall one evening getting the news that the UK Health Secretary contracted Covid-19 and that for me was an indication that things will soon be shut down. I wasn't wrong, within weeks we had gone into a global lockdown.

That night I was faced with a dilemma - continue to persevere, have faith or accept the harsh reality and retreat. After seeing the situation for what it was, I could not risk the health of my audience or pretend like all this chaos was not happening around us. I reached out to all our speakers and the team and told them the event was cancelled. It rested heavy on my heart because I am the kind of person that will keep my promise till the end, but in this case the situation was out of my hands. I cried that night in self-pity for all my hard work I put into making this event happen.

Organising a live event in a local region is stressful enough but doing it in a city you have never been in or have any connections in requires a different level of faith. The next day I announced to our audience that the event will not be going ahead. The outpour of support was overwhelming - so many women reached out to say that they were watching the situation unfold and praying for me and this event to go forth. I was vulnerable and able to accept defeat but in turn found the support and encouragement from my community. My comfort was knowing that I was not alone in this situation and that everyone around the world was dealing with their own unique challenges. Most of us were in deep uncertainty for our businesses, jobs, family settings, health and other things that were impacted by the pandemic. It gave me comfort knowing that we are all facing these unprecedented times together and navigating the situation the best way we all can. I was not alone, and so it was time to choose what course of action we would take. For me it was a moment of realisation of will we let this sink or find a way to swim? Will we sit and watch the situation unfold or lead the way through this situation? For me, it was the latter. I knew that my community needed guidance and support, they needed hope and encouragement. They needed the next steps to find a way through this. So, my idea to pivot came to me within days since cancelling our Atlanta event - we need to have a global virtual summit that will help women survive and thrive during this pandemic. So, I called it the Women Thrive Summit, an event to help women survive and thrive in business and life. The same week I shared a post in several Facebook groups reaching out for speakers from a wider network. To my surprise we had 100's of women respond to the call. Applications came pouring in, we had so many women interested to speak that we extended our event from 20 speakers to 34 speakers. Every day I was holding calls with women to hear their stories and it motivated me to persevere. We had gone through 100's of applications within a very short period of time and were quickly set up to host the event. In just 4 weeks we pivoted our live event and turned what would have been 250 people into a nearly 2,000 people event, from 8 speakers to 34 speakers.

During this summit I had the privilege to interview some of the most amazing women from all around the world and make an impact on a global scale. I realised that the pandemic has pushed people out of their comfort zones and allowed them to re-evaluate their lives. Many have gone on to quit their jobs, start new businesses, follow their life-long passions, write books, release courses and finally step into the life they always wanted to live. Being aligned to their true purpose. If the pandemic wasn't an awakening enough - I think on the global and personal level we all have had to go through a rebirth or some kind of transformation, because life as we knew it was gone.

For me this was a new chapter. The Women Thrive Summit was more than just an event - it was a joint effort between women with a mission to make an impact, to inspire, educate and lead other women. It became about women empowerment because only we women know the unique challenges other women go through in order to reach success. The pandemic showed just how much inequality there still is for women. How we are the primary caretakers at home and with the children and how much this is a sacrifice on our personal goals and dreams. By nature, women are givers and nurturers, and it comes naturally to most to be giving. But it comes at a cost of not serving ourselves. Through the many conversations with other women globally I realised that we must continue to make an impact with women because the more empowered and strong women are the more positive impact will be made globally. When women succeed, they not only succeed for themselves, but they also succeed for their families, for their communities, they give back and support others, not just financially but in making an impact. Women are incredibly empathetic, giving, loving and kind. We want to nurture and serve so, when women are empowered, they will make a ripple effect on this earth.

At the time this was one event - simply finding a way

forward after the inevitable knock back of the pandemic but what unfolded after, no one could anticipate. The post summit ripple effect was evident, the transformation in the women who attended the event. The transformation in the speakers who spoke at the event, everyone's confidence levels had gone up, women were pursuing their goals, showing up more confidently and being inspired to keep on going. For us, this became an annual event, year on year we had more than 2,000 attendees. In 2021 we had more than 40 international speakers, reached over 3 million views online, we were endorsed by the legendary and the most proclaimed motivational speaker Les Brown. Through our events we got to support and be endorsed by charities like The Global Fund for Women and The Female Lead Charity - whilst raising money and donating to women related causes. In 2021 we focused more on open forum conversations about diversity and inclusion, women empowerment, body confidence, age, gender and other issues facing our society.

On this journey I met women and men from all walks of life and realised that we all have struggles, we all have stories and experiences to share. Some are positive and others have been challenges and lessons, that can now be someone else's saving grace. Many people however, go a lifetime without sharing their stories with the world and take those experiences with them to the grave. It is the biggest regret of having lived a lifetime and not shared the gifts you have with the world. That is why I encourage every person to start sharing their authentic stories with the world. Be it in writing, spoken word, public speaking, writing a book or a memoir. If you're reading this book - you have read the stories of other women featured in this book - what made you feel inspired? What connected with you at a deeper level? These are the very same things that your readers or listeners could connect with you. Through the power of your story. What will you do after reading this book? How will you show up in the world?

For me showing up and sharing my voice and my story was not so easy. For years I struggled with speaking up. In fact, in my previous collaborative book - The Younger Self Letters I wrote about a time in my life when I lost my voice.

In my early 20's I completely lost my voice due to the trauma of a toxic relationship. After that I felt completely ripped of my confidence, my self-esteem, my identity and my voice. I was afraid to speak, and I had no idea who I was. This experience taught me that in life we can hit the lowest lows, lose it all and still find a way to build ourselves back up.

If I was able to lose my voice, my identity, my confidence and my business at the time and still find a way to not only rebuild my strength, but also become a speaker and build a platform for other speakers, I think there are many things you can do too that you have no idea of how capable you are.

The biggest dream killer is self-doubt and comfort zone. When you are comfortable and safe - there is no reason to go out there and fight a battle. If you are comfortable right now, I urge you to challenge yourself to get out of it as soon as you can. Do things that scare you or push you out of your comfort. The other is self-doubt - when we doubt ourselves, we don't move forward. We are stuck in analysis paralysis - dreaming but not doing because we don't know if we can. Because we fear either success or failure. But I can tell you - you will not know if you can or not until you try.

This goes for everything in life - your goals, your career, your business, adventure and even happiness. So many people feel unhappy and don't know why - because they are not willing to step outside their comfort zone and do something they have never done before. That is called living - not merely surviving and accepting your reality as it is.

So, what is next for us at the Women Thrive and Women in Business Community? I am pushing myself and those around me outside of their comfort zones. In 2021 we launched the

Women Thrive Magazine which scared the living daylights out of me. In 2022 we launched the Women Thrive magazine publishing platform that is the next Forbes for women. It is a magazine and self-publishing platform where women can share their voice. Where we together can take back our power in telling our stories. The media has never been too kind to entrepreneurial women who are making an incredible impact in the world. The media would rather focus on celebrity gossip and the headlines that sell, not real stories of real women making a difference in this world. So, it is time we claim our power back and have a place where women's voices are heard.

In 2022 we also launched our own Women Thrive TV Show - where women are able to debate important issues and topics of interest for entrepreneurial women. The Women Thrive is now a global Media Platform giving a voice to women to share their stories and empower other women globally. As one of my favourite quotes goes 'We cannot all succeed if half of us are held back' Malala Yousafzai.

BIO:

Raimonda Jankunaite is a serial entrepreneur, best selling author, international speaker, visibility coach and the founder of the Women in Business Club - international community for female entrepreneurs. In 2020 she also founded the Women Thrive Summit that is now an annual women empowerment event happening every March. The Women Thrive has now become a media platform that spotlights other women in business to share their voice and their stories through the various media platforms, including the Women Thrive Magazine, Podcast and a TV show.

www.womeninbusiness.club

2 9

FROM CATASTROPHE TO CALM

Neena Saith

I never set out to start my own business, it was not part of my plan – or at least, not that I knew of! But when I closed the door to my corporate career, another door opened that led me to start my own business. Based on how my corporate career affected my health I had developed a passion to help people find more balance in their lives and overcome stress and trauma related illnesses and pain that people are so prone to now. I'm now in the very fortunate position where I help other people be the best they can be by letting go of past traumas and stuck energy which is preventing them from thriving in life.

I'd spent 13 years working in the 'safe' environment of corporate companies. After studying for an MSc in Meteorology my first role was as a Weather Forecaster. However, it soon became clear that my body did not respond well to shift work and coupled to the lack of career prospects I looked for a new challenge which I found in the City of London at a Catastrophe Modelling company. Here I worked for 10 years, climbing the career ladder, gaining skills in Disaster Response,

Risk Management, Product Management, Product Marketing, and people management. I was in a senior role, earning a healthy salary and had a very positive career ahead of me.

So why change that?

I was extremely driven and ambitious and always had a focus on my next promotion and pay rise. Good at working under pressure and to tight deadlines, I was seemingly thriving in my job. That all changed in 2011 when I had my first child. I was taken aback by the emotion I felt, the deepest sense of love I had ever experienced but when partnered with high levels of stress driven by extreme tiredness, I found the situation hard to cope with. It was a whirlwind and an emotional rollercoaster – one that I certainly wasn't prepared for! I went back to work nine months later, working full time with an attitude of determination to keep my career and be a good Mum. It soon became apparent to me that the right balance was hard to achieve and within a year, there I was, sat in my boss's office with tears streaming down my face, feeling totally burnt out, physically, emotionally and mentally.

We adjusted my working hours and the focus of my role shifted but my health was well under par. I found myself with a constant stream of colds, often developing into tonsillitis and in September 2013 I had my tonsils taken out. A month or two later, whilst my immune system felt stronger, I started to experience severe pain in my neck and shoulders. After trying all sorts of physical solutions such as changing pillows, mattresses, desk position, I finally came to the realisation that the pain I was experiencing was linked to my emotions. This was a lightbulb moment for me and sent me on a path to start exploring 'out of the box' solutions to get the root of my pain. I was convinced that it must be possible to do so and was not willing to accept living with pain.

A regular practise of meditation helped me to build a greater sense of awareness of myself and what felt like a stronger core, deep within me. Without a doubt, this enhanced my ability to cope with stress and I found myself reacting much more calmly to situations that may have otherwise caused anger or upset.

It did not solve the physical pain but it felt like it was striping away layers of stress.

The breakthrough for my pain finally came when I enrolled myself on an Energy Healing course. For those of you who have not come across Energy Healing before, the therapy works with the subtle flow of energy throughout the body. It is a very gentle yet powerful natural approach to healing physical, emotional and mental conditions. It can be particularly effective for pain in the body, stress, anxiety, emotional turmoil and coping with challenging times.

Not only did my pain wash away that weekend, like some sort of miracle, but by starting to build an understanding of the energy system and how crucial it is to our health and everyday life, it helped me feel more in control and gave me hope that it was possible to live pain free, have an abundance of energy, feel positive and enthusiastic again. I was totally blown away by the amazing impacts on how I felt on all levels, though my scientific brain was constantly questioning it, I continued to learn more and understand the concept of the energy body and how it impacts your health and wellbeing. After all, as Albert Einstein said "everything is energy, and that's all there is to it".

Life started getting better and better and although I didn't feel the same 'spark' for my work as I did when I started out, I generally felt happier and healthier. But not long after, my world came crashing down again when I miscarried a baby at 9½ weeks. This was like an earthquake, shattering my husband and I completely, our hopes and dreams of expanding our family were crushed. I took a few days off work but did not tell anyone what had happened. A few months later I fell pregnant again but sadly miscarried for a second time – it felt like another earthquake turning our world upside down and this time taking me to a tipping point. I sobbed down the phone to my boss to explain what happened and then took myself off to a healer that helped me feel more grounded, calm and clear again. At this point I took the decision to press the pause button and requested to take some time off work.

When I stepped back from work and took a proper break, I started to see the wood through the trees. As I was trying to make the decision whether to go back to work at all, I was given what was probably some of the soundest advice I've ever been given. "Listen to your body" I was told, by two different people. Whilst this was what I had started to do over the last couple of years, at this point I leaned into what my body was telling me even further. On a train trip into London to visit the office and 'keep in touch', I was aware of how tense my body had become and so I knew at that point that going back to work wasn't the right thing to do. My husband fully backed me when I took what felt like a very brave decision to leave my safe corporate role, having been financially independent and the main bread winner for some time. I had no idea *what* I was going to do but knew that I needed to stop and focus on motherhood. It felt very daunting and for quite some time felt rather 'lost' but over-time I began to put into practise the skills I'd learned on the energy healing courses, practising on friends and family. With gentle encouragement from others, in 2016 I got myself insured, found a therapy room to practise from and off I went. It was a very slow start with a big dose of fear and imposter syndrome looming over me but with encouragement and healing from others, I was able to overcome these.

It never ceases to amaze me what is possible when working with the energy system. I have seen incredible changes to people, myself included and I will passionately continue to raise awareness of this very gentle yet powerful approach to healing.

As with any business, I am continuing to evolve in terms of how I work and who I work with. I have helped people with a wide range of conditions, ranging from sporting injuries and aches and pains to Post Traumatic Stress Disorder, anxiety and depression. What has become very clear to me is that healing requires a multi pronged approach, not just looking at the physical problem but identifying and healing the underlying emotions. Energy healing does this in such a gentle way so that people who have suffered deep traumas, do not have to relive these events in order to release them.

Ultimately my goal is to help others reconnect with themselves and their own healing abilities, so they are enabled to bring themselves back to a place of balance when life events knock them out of kilter. When I reflect back on my own journey, one of the biggest lessons for me is about selfcare. Once my first child came along, I gave myself very little nurturing and care. I thought it was only right to be putting other people's needs before my own but the reality is, this couldn't be further from the truth and my body had to give me a big wake up call to come to this realisation. If I can help others understand only this, then that feels like a big win to me. To be able to help someone along their own healing journey is nothing but an honour.

BIO:

I discovered energy healing at a time in my life when 'stress' had taken a strong hold. I was working hard in the corporate world and raising a family which was taking a toll on my physical and mental health. Having tried numerous therapies I discovered energy healing and set out on a journey to learn techniques to help self-heal.

Coming from a science background I was sceptical at first and found the non-touch aspect of the healing hard to swallow. However, there was no questioning the benefits I started to feel and within no time at all my neck pain disappeared, my energy levels rose and I started to feel much more resilient both physically and mentally. As I continued to learn, practise and validate what was being taught it became very clear to me that our energy system plays a key role in our health and well-being. I am now passionate about helping others improve their health using these wonderful complementary therapies.

www.neenashealing.com

30
WHAT THE HELL AM I DOING WITH MY LIFE?

Patricia Lohan

That's what I was thinking as I was cycling around Dublin on a borrowed bicycle back when I was a single sound healer and yoga teacher - "What the hell am I doing with my life?".

Some days I was earning as little as €5 a day. Most days I was sad about not finding love. I was working hard on myself and my business, reading self-help books, saying mantras, writing affirmations, and buying personal development courses. But I was still stuck, worrying about money, and having no luck in the love department. It was hard. My vision for my life was just so much... *bigger*. I felt like I was playing small just teaching yoga, doing sound healings, and selling knick-knacks I'd bought in India, while longing to have an amazing business, live somewhere nice, and break away from the 'smaller' version of me. I just couldn't figure out what to do, or how to break through.

Have you been here yourself?

How do you go from there, to attracting a husband and soulmate, turning your passion into a multi six-figure success, and becoming a role model to thousands of women around the globe?

The game-changer for me - *in every part of my life* - was Feng Shui.

I was 15 when I got my first Feng Shui book and I've always loved it. I grew up with entrepreneurial parents who worked all the time, running their businesses. All I ever knew was business, and I always had a job, right from the age of 7 or 8. As far back as I can remember, they ran restaurants, pubs, guesthouses, and hotels. When I was 18 years old, we were running a small hotel. I brought a Feng Shui expert to Galway, my home town, to Feng Shui my parents' new house. I remember believing at the time, "Feng Shui is really good for business", and convincing my parents to hire her!

Then life took me on a very different path where I 'forgot' about my passion for Feng Shui - I studied Business and Marketing and ended up back in my hometown working in the family businesses. After eight years, I decided to quit and move to India to become a yoga teacher. This was the best decision of my life and the beginning of a spiritual journey I could never have imagined.

My body opened up, my mind opened up, suddenly I was reading oracles cards for people, doing healings and being asked, what are you going to do with those magic hands? India opened me up and tapped me into the source. I stepped away from the old me and into a new more magical lighter version of myself.

When I returned back to Ireland from India, I was guided to move to Dublin - a fresh new start, I had no idea what I was going to do with my life for work or money. I couldn't afford to live alone, so I slept in a friend's spare room and borrowed another friend's bicycle to get around. I was grateful for my friend's apartment, for my family, and for my deep desire to make a difference in the world, even though I wasn't sure how I would do that. I knew I wanted to earn more money and find my soulmate, so I trusted the process - and my circumstances started to change

I was starting from scratch. I wondered if I'd ever move abroad, meet 'the one' or be capable of earning more than €5 in a day. Despite being immersed in personal development, I couldn't figure out why I couldn't break through and just be successful. Despite my sunny spirit, I was caught in a daily pattern of fear, and that had to go! I was single. I was broke. It seemed like the perfect time to give Feng Shui another try.

Instead of focusing on what I didn't have, I spent my energy showing gratitude for everything I did have, and incredible things started happening. For one, I manifested my dream apartment by writing a wish list and trusting the process. I started to see how important it was to hold an intention in my mind.

My new home needed to focus on my current vision and there was only one way I knew to make that happen. Feng Shui. I started implementing Feng Shui as soon as I moved in, digging out the books I had been given on my 15th birthday, removing negative energy, and creating my own remedy for success.

Determined to attract the right person, I Feng Shui-ed my bedroom for love. I met Ken a couple of months later, at a fire-walk, and we've been together for over 8 years. Soon after I met Ken, my now-husband, he told me he had Feng-Shui-ed his bedroom for love too. As coincidence upon coincidence came, I finally saw that Feng Shui *was* the answer... and it was my chance.

After seeing my own results I realised, I could use this tool for sooo much more in my life! I followed my heart to blend my healing practices with Feng Shui. I decided to dig into it and become a devoted student of this ancient art.

As I transformed the energy of our home, our life quickly transformed too: we manifested a 6 figure windfall, attracted

COMPILED BY TRUDY SIMMONS

more ideal clients, incredible opportunities flowed in like being featured in the New York Times, Forbes and National TV interviews - but the best bit has been seeing the same happen for my clients.

As I dived in deeper I reflected on the homes I lived in, I had so many realisations, my family and I moved house many times growing up. There was one house in particular where our personal family life literally fell apart. My family's business was booming but behind the scenes personally - It was bad for people. We were a normal, fairly happy family up until that point . Once we moved in, my Mum got really sick, we had lots of legal issues, my sister got really ill. It was truly a tough house to live in, life did not flow easil. But when we moved out, lots of the issues we had been having, disappeared. I realised it wasn't the occupants, it was the house. This ignited my desire to help women in the same situation and help people transform this energy just like Gael.

'This was supposed to be our dream house - but our lives have started falling apart since we moved in. This is my last resort"

When I read these words, my heart literally was torn in half. I was so upset for my client. She was at her wits' end and didn't know what to do. Her marriage was on the verge of divorce, her children didn't want to come home, and her business was barely scraping by. Things seemed desperate and she needed help quickly! The personality of her house was bad for people and for money.

I created her customised report for her house. She did absolutely everything I suggested and within weeks of implementing the suggested remedies, things started to turn around. Her relationship started blossoming again, her kids started to want to come home, life started to flow and her business took off she had her first 6 figure year in business from $19,000 (she had been working SO hard on her business but wasn't able to reap the rewards as her house was blocking that energy).

Turning people's lives around, making life easier, eliminating the struggle. This is my why and that's exactly what I do for my clients . The scary thing is without knowing it, your home is impacting whatever frustrations (financial, health, relationship, family, career or business) you are having in your life and it is limiting your potential to shine.

Now, I've helped hundreds of women around the world transform their lives by magnetising their homes through the practice of Feng Shui. My clients are women who come from all walks of life - women just like you. These women have called amazing things into their lives, mind blowing business successes, national media attention, babies conceived, incredible financial abundance, to just more flow and ease in their lives. Through working with me to transform the energy of their homes, they made their dreams come to reality.

I know there are more people out there who are still going through what I was feeling back in Dublin or like Gael. If it sounds anything like you, you're in the right place. You may have done lots of personal development work, journaling, tapping, praying, NLP, the works. You've created a vision board that still isn't becoming a reality, maybe you're making money but struggling to do so, having relationships that are tense, frustrating, or non-existent. Well, I am overjoyed to be able to share Feng Shui with you.

You are about to embark on a journey to enhance your home so that it supports you in creating happiness, health, and wealth in your life. You can have all the blessings, the joy, and the abundance you desire. It all starts at home.

If you're doing good but you've hit a plateau. Or, you're doing the work but not getting the results. Perhaps you're looking at the others' success and wondering, "is any of this actually working?" Here's the good news: it IS working, BUT it's likely your house isn't matching your newly magnetised energy.

While YOU up-levelled yourself, your home hasn't -- and

that's the thing that's holding you back. You have the power to harness your home's magnetic energy to call in anything you want... you simply have to set it up to be in harmony with your desires. That's what Feng Shui can do for you. Sounds good? Yes!

So... What is Feng Shui? Feng Shui fung shu.. It doesn't matter how you pronounce it.. it's nothing to be scared off (pinky promise). Feng Shui has been around for more than 5,000 years - So it's a time tested technique!There are a lot of misconceptions out there about what Feng Shui involves...Feng Shui is not about moving furniture around, knocking walls, making structural changes, hanging lucky trinkets and getting rid of mirrors. I'll never tell you to move house! To be totally honest, I don't care where your couch is! I'm not going to tell you to get rid of all your favourite things and paint your house white.Feng Shui is not about superstition or superstitious practices. Feng Shui isn't about interior design (even the most stunning dream home could be bad feng shui!). Feng Shui isn't just for the 'hippies' and woo woo peeps...

Feng Shui isn't only for Huge Companies (all whole foods have been feng shui'd) Famous Movie Stars, Hollywood Directors, Billionaire Entrepreneurs (who all use it) ... BUT just like those Billionaire Entrepreneurs you can have the success that they are having using Feng Shui. No matter what type of house, apartment or tiny home you live in - you can use Feng Shui to move to the next level and beyond the truth is ANYONE in any type of house, apartment or mobile home can use it to improve their lives.

Feng Shui is acupuncture for your home.

Good news -- you don't need to believe in Feng Shui for it to work!

BIO:

Patricia Lohan is a Feng Shui expert, manifesting magnet, alchemist, healer and real-life Irish Celtic Shaman. She is the creator of PowerHouse Feng Shui and author of *The Happy Home: A Guide To Creating A Happy, Healthy, Wealthy Life.* Thousands of people across the globe have been helped by Patricia to embrace Feng Shui and create incredible transformations in their businesses, homes and lives. Patricia has been featured in media around the world, including *The New York Times, CNN, Forbes, The New York Post, Essence, Mind Body Green,* and *Elephant Journal.*

www.patricialohan.com

ABOUT THE DAISY CHAIN GROUP

Trudy Simmons started The Daisy Chain Group in 2010. It was started to support and encourage businesswomen to have a safe space to share their journeys, to grow their businesses and to be seen and heard in their endeavours.

Since its inception, the concept has grown to include platforms for women to find their voice and become more visible in lots of different ways. Whether it is attending online networking events, committing to co-working time together, learning from experts in masterclasses or investing in monthly business coaching to boost your accountability and momentum, we all need to find the space to work ON our businesses.

If you have a story to share, come and be a part of the Shine On You Crazy Daisy book series and share your story, or be on the Shine On You Crazy Daisy Podcast to give your story gravitas and hear it in your own voice.

Trudy is known for her engaged communities on Facebook – The Hampshire Women's Business Group (for local businesswomen) and The International Women's Business Group (for any businesswoman that wants or has a global audience).

HAVING FUN in your business is a core value of The Daisy

Chain Group. Having fun and TAKING ACTION is what builds you AND your business.

You can find The Daisy Chain Group here:

www.thedaisychaingroup.com

https://www.facebook.com/daisychaingroup

https://www.instagram.com/daisychaingroup/

https://www.linkedin.com/in/trudysimmons/

You can find The Daisy Chain Group communities here:

https://www.facebook.com/groups/hampshirewomensbusiness

https://www.facebook.com/groups/internationalwomensbusiness

You can find our services here:

Shine On You Crazy Daisy Membership - https://www.thedaisychaingroup.com/shine-on-you-crazy-daisy-membership

You can listen to the Shine On You Crazy Daisy Podcast here:

https://www.thedaisychaingroup.com/podcasts/shine-on-you-crazy-daisy

EVERY TIME YOU BUY FROM A SMALL BUSINESS, THEY DO A HAPPY DANCE!

PLEASE SUPPORT THE BUSINESSES IN THIS BOOK.

CHARITY LINK

10% of the profits from this book will be donated to Healthcare Workers' Foundation Family Fund. The fund will support the children and families of healthcare workers who have passed due to Covid-19. To donate or support this incredible charity, please go to this link

www.healthcareworkersfoundation.org

OTHER BOOKS

AVAILABLE NOW

Shine On You Crazy Daisy – Volume 1
Shine On You Crazy Daisy – Volume 2
Shine On You Crazy Daisy – Volume 3

Available on Amazon, iBook and in all good bookshops.

COMING SOON

Shine On You Crazy Daisy – Volume 5

Available in March 2022 – more stories, more inspiration, more motivation to get out there and do what you WANT to do with your business.

We are all in this together.

Lightning Source UK Ltd.
Milton Keynes UK
UKHW020643200222
398879UK00006B/183